At Issue

FR

Nuclear and Toxic Waste

Other Books in the At Issue Series:

At Issue

Nuclear and Toxic Waste

Stefan Kiesbye, Book Editor

Yolo County Library
226 Buckeye Street
Woodland, CA 95695
530-666-8005

GREENHAVEN PRESS
A part of Gale, Cengage Learning

GALE
CENGAGE Learning

Detroit • New York • San Francisco • New Haven, Conn • Waterville, Maine • London

Christine Nasso, *Publisher*
Elizabeth Des Chenes, *Managing Editor*

© 2010 Greenhaven Press, a part of Gale, Cengage Learning.

Gale and Greenhaven Press are registered trademarks used herein under license.

For more information, contact:
Greenhaven Press
27500 Drake Rd.
Farmington Hills, MI 48331-3535
Or you can visit our Internet site at gale.cengage.com

ALL RIGHTS RESERVED.
No part of this work covered by the copyright herein may be reproduced, transmitted, stored, or used in any form or by any means graphic, electronic, or mechanical, including but not limited to photocopying, recording, scanning, digitizing, taping, Web distribution, information networks, or information storage and retrieval systems, except as permitted under Section 107 or 108 of the 1976 United States Copyright Act, without the prior written permission of the publisher.

For product information and technology assistance, contact us at

Gale Customer Support, 1-800-877-4253
For permission to use material from this text or product, submit all requests online at www.cengage.com/permissions

Further permissions questions can be e-mailed to permissionrequest@cengage.com

Articles in Greenhaven Press anthologies are often edited for length to meet page requirements. In addition, original titles of these works are changed to clearly present the main thesis and to explicitly indicate the author's opinion. Every effort is made to ensure that Greenhaven Press accurately reflects the original intent of the authors. Every effort has been made to trace the owners of copyrighted material.

Cover image © Debra Hughes 2007. Used under license from Shutterstock.com.

LIBRARY OF CONGRESS CATALOGING-IN-PUBLICATION DATA

Nuclear and toxic waste / Stefan Kiesbye, book editor.
    p. cm. -- (At issue)
Includes bibliographical references and index.
ISBN 978-0-7377-4681-5 (hardcover)
ISBN 978-0-7377-4682-2 (pbk.)
1. Radioactive wastes--Juvenile literature. 2. Hazardous wastes--Juvenile litera-
ture. I. Kiesbye, Stefan.
TD898.N78 2010
363.72'89--dc22

                                                              2009038709

Printed in the United States of America
1 2 3 4 5 6 7 14 13 12 11 10

Contents

Introduction

Some catastrophes are so encompassing as to garner national and international attention. The *Exxon Valdez* disaster of March 24, 1989, when an oil tanker bound for Long Beach, California, hit Prince William Sound's Bligh Reef and spilled an estimated minimum 10.8 million U.S. gallons (40.9 million liters) of crude oil, is one of them. The Love Canal toxic waste scandal is another. Love Canal, a neighborhood in Niagara Falls, New York, gained international attention and notoriety in the late 1970s, when it was discovered that 21,000 tons of toxic waste had been buried there by Hooker Chemical. The damage to the environment, wildlife, and humans was extensive in both cases, and these incidents continue to represent the environmental and human damage that large-scale disasters can produce.

Yet the damages caused by nuclear and toxic waste are not always as dramatic as a leaking nuclear reactor or an oil tanker's shipwreck. Many communities around the world are exposed to toxic waste, often without knowing it.

In 1999, *Environment California* wrote that, "[i]n tests of a widely-used home fertilizer sold throughout California, every sample exceeded federal criteria for classification as hazardous waste, according to an analysis conducted for the California Public Interest Research Group (CALPIRG) and the Environmental Working Group (EWG)." Tests focusing on commercial fertilizers proved even more disastrous. "State data analyzed by CALPIRG and EWG show that more than one-sixth of the commercial fertilizers tested by the California Department of Food and Agriculture (CDFA) exceeded federal hazardous waste criteria for heavy metals including lead and arsenic. Between 1994 and 1998, CDFA tested more than 250 samples of commercial (mostly agricultural use) fertilizer products for lead, arsenic and cadmium, a highly toxic and carcinogenic element. Thirteen percent of the cadmium tainted samples exceeded hazardous waste criteria, as did seven percent of the lead-containing samples and two percent of the arsenic-containing samples."

On September 2, 2002, ABC News reported that "drinking water in a Wauconda, Ill., subdivision ha[d] become contaminated with a vinyl chloride, a suspected cancer-causing agent, and residents [were] demanding the EPA [Environmental Protection Agency] clean up the problem." Residents had first become aware of the contamination a year earlier, but nothing had been done by the authorities. "The chemical is believed to have leaked from an abandoned landfill about a quarter mile away and so far has contaminated the well water used by as many as 120 homes in the subdivision," the network reported at that time. The landfill had been used for storing toxic waste since 1982.

On December 6, 2007, *Natural News* editor Mike Adams reported on the Web site MrGreenBiz.com that "[f]iring ranges expose the environment and the ecosystem to lead pollution caused by the presence of lead in ammunition projectiles. This makes lead pollution a major concern for the public. When these bullets are fired, they emit lead particles that are then inhaled, absorbed into the skin or disposed of in community landfill facilities. Currently, very few cities are taking action to reduce the health threat and environmental burden of lead bullets. Similar to mercury, lead is both a heavy metal and a potent neurotoxin that builds up over time in bones and soft tissue. Lead particles, dust and gases are especially present at shooting ranges because of the lead components contained in most bullets. Unless the ammunition is specifically manufactured to be lead-free, it is always made with lead."

Adams estimated that there are about "8,000 public and private recreational shooting ranges" and that they are contaminated with tons of lead, posing a significant health risk to users and nonusers alike, as well as to wildlife. These sites are neglected toxic waste sites, and it would cost "millions to clean them up." In Adams's words, "Ducks and geese have been found poisoned in lakes polluted by lead shot. Shooting ranges could be declared hazardous waste sites by the Environmental Protection Agency when [those businesses] are shut down."

Even after potential health risks have been discovered, the ways in which to clean up sites and where to dispose of the toxic waste are hotly debated issues. Many citizens are wary of the prospect of housing a waste disposal site in their neighborhood, and many speak out against merely shifting a waste problem in one city or state to the next. From producing hazardous materials and byproducts to disposing of them, from finding new, safe energies to storing nuclear waste—the world faces tough challenges in times of ever-increasing pollution, a still-increasing demand for energy, and an environment that is more than ever at risk.

1

Nuclear Waste Is a Critical Threat

Greenpeace

Greenpeace is an international nongovernmental organization for the protection and conservation of the environment.

Nuclear waste is and will remain a serious problem for mankind. Not only do leaks and spills threaten the environment, but so far no satisfying long-term solution for waste storage has been found. In addition, nuclear waste may be used to build weapons. And increasingly, storage facilities and reactors have to be regarded as targets for possible terrorist attacks.

The existing UK [United Kingdom] nuclear facilities will leave us a legacy of half a million tonnes of nuclear waste—and some of this will remain as a threat to human health and the environment for hundreds of thousands of years.

There is no final disposal option for the more radioactive intermediate and high level wastes or spent fuel in the UK. NIREX [Nuclear Industry Radioactive Waste Executive], the agency charged originally with building a disposal dump for waste, has said that it does not believe a waste site will be available for at least the next 25–40 years. Many observers be-

Greenpeace, "Nuclear Waste Presents a Critical Problem," *Greenpeace.org*, July 20, 2005. Reproduced by permission.

lieve that the only credible option currently available is to keep the waste in above ground stores where it can be monitored and retrieved if necessary.

Leaks and Spills

In the meantime, the amount of waste continues to grow. It was revealed recently that a massive 18 million cubic metres of soil and rubble have been contaminated by leaks, spills and discharges from 30 nuclear sites across the UK over the past 60 years. This figure could double when the full extent of the problem is known. Only 1.9 million cubic metres of low-level radioactive waste had been declared in an earlier official inventory.

Building ten more plants would significantly increase the waste problem—particularly for the most hazardous and radioactive wastes. According to the Committee on Radioactive Waste Management (CoRWM): 'The quantity of spent fuel requiring management could increase significantly, by *approximately double*, if say 10 new nuclear power stations were to be built and assuming this fuel were not reprocessed' (emphasis added), if the spent fuel [were] reprocessed it would add even more to the UK's stockpile of weapons-usable plutonium and the already large amounts of extremely radioactive liquid waste. There are already major difficulties in addressing the problem of high-level liquid waste at Sellafield [a nuclear processing site].

In promotional documents for the AP1000 [a nuclear plant by Westinghouse] published by the nuclear industry, the question of waste management is not fully answered. Industry plans for dealing with the additional spent fuel from new reactors is no more sophisticated than creating ground-level stores where the fuel rods will be kept on site for 100 years—further increasing the number of terrorist targets.

An expansion of the nuclear industry would further increase risks from terrorism and proliferation of nuclear weapons.

The Nuclear Industry Is a Potential Terrorist Target

One of the fundamental and insoluble problems of nuclear power is the hazard posed by the radioactive materials it produces—some of which can be used in nuclear weapons and all of which can be used in so-called 'dirty bombs'. This means that sites containing nuclear materials or nuclear transports are very attractive targets for terrorists. After the 11 September [2001] terrorist attack on the World Trade Centre in New York, the nuclear industry conceded that nuclear power plants, nuclear waste and spent fuel transports, and waste facilities should be regarded as potential targets.

The impacts of a terrorist attack on a nuclear power reactor would of course be dependent on how much radioactive material was released and the plant's location (facilities near large centres of population would mean more people would be at risk). A recent study in the US put the health impacts of an attack on a reactor at 44,000 immediate fatalities with 500,000 long-term health impacts, including cancers. Nuclear facilities and transports also provide targets for terrorists wanting to steal nuclear materials to use in a low-grade nuclear bomb or a 'dirty bomb'.

An expansion of the nuclear industry would further increase risks from terrorism and proliferation of nuclear weapons.

Worryingly, the global nuclear watchdog, the International Atomic Energy Authority (IAEA), has had to appeal for money to update its computer system so it can more effectively track nuclear materials, admitting that the current system is outdated and is not modern enough for effective inspections. The UK's Office of Civil Nuclear Security has recently decided to post armed police around all the nuclear reactor sites in the UK—underlining the security risk of these sites.

An International Nuclear Industry Fuels Weapons Proliferation

Any effective energy solution to climate change must be able to be applied internationally. The expansion of nuclear power for electricity generation will result in the spread of dual-use (civil and military) nuclear material and technology around the world.

The spread of nuclear technologies and materials internationally is causing increasing concern—it is widely acknowledged that a number of nuclear weapons programmes have started from supposedly civil nuclear operations. The current tensions around Iran's civil nuclear programme are a good illustration of how politically sensitive this issue has become.

So those who are promoting nuclear power as an answer to climate change do so knowing they are not only encouraging the export of an environmentally hazardous technology, but also the wherewithal to embark on a nuclear weapons programme. Few of them have seriously addressed this major issue.

2

The Problem of Nuclear Waste Storage May Be Overcome

Jim Al-Khalili

Jim Al-Khalili is professor of physics, and professor of the public engagement in science, at the University of Surrey. He is the 2007 recipient of the Royal Society Michael Faraday prize for science communication. In 2007 he presented a three-part documentary series, called Atom, *about the history of understanding of the atom and atomic physics.*

With energy demand at a historic high and with no clean and efficient alternatives, nuclear energy is the best possible solution. And though current waste storage is unpopular with the public, a new process called transmutation can turn atomic waste into less hazardous material, while also generating energy. New solutions to make nuclear energy safer are on the horizon, if only the atomic industry and governments worldwide decide to fund further research.

With all things wizardly being topical, what better time to examine one of the practical skills that every self respecting wizard should master: alchemy? But this near-magical ability to turn base metals into gold is not confined to fiction. The quest for the so-called philosopher's stone that has the power to transmute one substance into another has been the obsession of many great thinkers throughout history. The wealth and power that would come to anyone who mastered

Jim Al-Khalili, "Nuclear Waste Is Hardly a Worry When the Climate Change Threat Is so Urgent," *The Guardian*, July 26, 2007. Copyright © Guardian News & Media Ltd 2007. Reproduced by permission.

alchemy seduced many great scientists and philosophers, including Isaac Newton, Robert Boyle and John Locke. All tried to change one element into another, and all failed.

Then in 1919, the secret of alchemy was finally revealed in the physics department at Manchester University. The world's first successful alchemist was the New Zealand scientist and Nobel prize winner Ernest Rutherford, and his discovery was almost accidental. It began when one of his students noticed that when radioactive materials such as radium were placed in a sealed box of air, small amounts of hydrogen, which doesn't exist in ordinary air, began to mysteriously appear. Rutherford realised that in the presence of the powerful radioactive rays, nitrogen, which makes up more than three-quarters of the air we breathe, turns into two other gases—hydrogen and oxygen.

Here we are trying to figure out how to avert the disaster of climate change now, and yet the long-term problem of nuclear waste still worries us.

The alpha particles being produced by the radium were embedding themselves within the nuclei of nitrogen atoms while knocking out single protons. What remained was an oxygen nucleus, while the protons themselves were actually nuclei of hydrogen. All that is needed then is for these nuclei to accumulate the requisite number of electrons and they become atoms of the respective gases. Today, changing one element into another through such nuclear reactions is routine. What is exciting, and yet not widely known, is that such subatomic alchemy might end up playing a vital part in the way we produce clean energy in the future.

A loose interpretation of the second law of thermodynamics is that "there is no such thing as a free lunch". And so it is with electrical energy production. If you burn fossil fuels, you generate C02; if you build dams, you destroy the ecology of entire valleys. Nuclear power is no exception. If you carry out controlled fission in a nuclear power station, you get long-lived radioactive waste, and that poses a long-term hazard to the environment unless it is dealt with properly. This has justifiably caused concern among many who would otherwise welcome nuclear power as a source of clean, carbon-free energy.

The favoured option is to store the treated and vitrified waste in deep geological repositories. Understandably, people don't want this in their backyard, not least because material such as plutonium remains radioactive for tens of thousands of years. In a democracy, in the throes of deciding its future energy policy, such concerns are a serious issue. I find this a very strange concern: here we are trying to figure out how to avert the disaster of climate change now, and yet the long-term problem of nuclear waste still worries us. Human civilisation started less than 10,000 years ago, so to worry whether we'll be technologically advanced enough to deal with this buried waste thousands of years in the future, assuming we survive climate change, is utterly irrational. And, what if there was a way to incinerate the nuclear waste, destroying nearly all that plutonium and dramatically reducing the need for long-term storage?

---

*If we are going to avert the disasters of climate change
... we are going to have to continue our reliance on
nuclear energy.*

One such strategy is known as accelerator-driven transmutation. The basic idea is to place the radioactive material in a machine and smash it up into much more stable products, with shorter half-lives using a beam of high-energy subatomic particles. The waste would still need to be stored, but would be much less hazardous. At the same time, the process of transmutation would eliminate other biologically toxic products that exist in "normal" nuclear waste.

The real beauty of the process is that it could generate more energy than is pumped in. The heat generated by splitting the waste nuclei can be used to generate electricity, part of which is used to run the accelerator and the rest fed into the national grid. The failsafe mechanism is that when the beam is turned off, the reaction stops. This type of plant is known as an "energy amplifier" and the idea has been around since the 1990s.

So how feasible is this ability to transmute our nuclear waste? More important, why is no one talking about it? After all, the nuclear waste problem is seen as the major obstacle stopping many people from embracing nuclear power as one of the key ingredients in carbon-free energy generation. It is a source of deep concern that so many people still believe we can slash our reliance on coal and gas solely through renewable sources, such as wind and solar, along with energy conservation in buildings. These are all vital, but if we are going to avert the disasters of climate change while enjoying the standard of living that most in the west would be unwilling to give up, we are going to have to continue our reliance on nuclear energy. If transmutation could be made to work, it would go a long way towards helping the world come to terms with it. Beyond this timescale, we are now finally and genuinely optimistic that the ultimate energy source will come online: nuclear fusion. But that's another story.

France has a well-funded programme of research looking into transmutation. There are also initiatives in the US, Russia, Switzerland, Italy and Japan, which the UK government continues to "monitor". The reason no one has perfected the technology yet is that while in theory it should work, we still do not know exactly what the final transmutation products will be, and in what proportions. The scientific community has to understand the science involved and the technology needed, its practicalities and potential impacts. This takes years. The US and Europe have produced roadmaps of timescales of 20 to 35 years. Unfortunately, the nuclear industry does not see transmutation as economically viable, and the onus is therefore on us to urge governments to act.

Many experts argue that while transmutation is a feasible future technology, there are several other options available too. The most widely touted is to use what is a called a fast-breeder reactor that would re-use the nuclear fuel over and over again until all the plutonium is burned up. Another option many nations are looking into is to use thorium as the basic nuclear fuel. It is more abundant in nature than uranium, and much less radioactive material is produced compared with uranium fuel cycles.

With all these possible options for coping with nuclear waste it is disappointing that what little public debate there has been in the UK seems to have been aimed at answering the question of "should we" rather than the technological question of "could we". The answer to the latter question is only likely to be found in a multidisciplinary effort involving scientists from a wide range of fields. Then the philosopher's stone will be within our grasp once more.

3

There Is No Credible Solution to the Nuclear Waste Problem

Mary Olson

Mary Olson is director of the Southeast Office of the Nuclear Information and Resource Service (NIRS) in Asheville, North Carolina.

Storing nuclear waste in centralized locations has so far proved futile and dangerous because sites chosen by the government are not safe, and transporting the dangerous material could have catastrophic results. Reprocessing waste, however, produces weapons-usable plutonium, and could at best lead to a renewed nuclear arms race, and at worst, enable developing and unstable nations to produce nuclear weapons.

Splitting atoms to make electricity has created an enormous problem: waste containing 95% of the toxic radioactivity produced during the Atomic Age. Nuclear weapons production, industrial activity, research and medicine combined, create only 5% of this problem.

Every nuclear power reactor annually generates 20–30 tons of high-level nuclear waste since the irradiated [exposed to radiation] fuel itself is the waste when removed from the reactor core. Like fuel, the waste is a solid ceramic pellet, stacked inside a thin metal tube or "cladding." In addition to residual uranium, the waste is about 1% plutonium that is formed inside the fuel rods by the fission reactor. The waste also con-

Mary Olson, *NIRS Energy Fact Sheet: Reprocessing Is NOT the 'Solution' to the Nuclear Waste Problem*, Asheville, NC: Nuclear Information and Resource Service, 2006. Updated June 2009. Reproduced by permission.

tains about 5% highly radioactive fission [splitting a large atomic nucleus in half] products like cesium, strontium and iodine, making it millions of times more radioactive than "fresh" uranium fuel. Unshielded, it delivers a lethal dose in seconds and will remain a hazard for at least 12,000 human generations.

No End in Site

High-level waste is piling up at reactor sites, stored outside of containment in pools, and in large dry containers called casks. A growing security threat, storage expansion has been repeatedly approved to enable continued reactor operation, and therefore continued nuclear waste production, making risks greater. Now new reactors are being proposed, even though there is no credible solution for the approximately 120,000 tons of waste the first generation of reactors will produce.

Like fuel, the [nuclear] waste is a solid ceramic pellet, stacked inside a thin metal tube or "cladding."

The U.S. Department of Energy (DOE) has devoted nearly 20 years to the development of a high-level dump at Yucca Mountain, a geologically unstable, sacred site of the Western Shoshone people in Nevada. The State of Nevada and the Shoshone Nation have vigorously opposed this dump. Growing evidence substantiates that the Yucca site will fail in the fundamental goal of a repository: to isolate radioactivity from our environment. A series of proposed centralized storage sites—several on Indian Reservations—have been prevented by ardent public opposition. Any centralization of this waste, including a reprocessing site, would trigger a "Mobile Chernobyl"—the largest nuclear waste shipping campaign in history—with so many transport miles that accidents are inevitable and security is an oxymoron.

Disregarding Hard-Won Wisdom

A 2004 [George W.] Bush / [Dick] Cheney administration initiative reversed over 30 years of extraordinarily rare common sense in nuclear policy. In the 1970s it was decided that irradiated fuel, and the plutonium it contains, should be treated as *waste*—not as a resource. This was in part due to the catastrophic failure after only a few years of operation at West Valley, New York—the only commercial reprocessing site to operate in the U.S. West Valley's reprocessing mess is still not cleaned up—and the projected cost at that site is now over $9 billion.

Reprocessing creates stockpiles of nuclear weapons-usable plutonium, and is unviable without large taxpayer subsidies.

Every reprocessing site (France, UK, Russia and Japan have the largest sites) is an environmental catastrophe, with massive releases of radioactivity to air, land and water; high worker radiation exposures; and residues that are harder to handle than the terrible waste it begins with. Reprocessing creates stockpiles of nuclear weapons-usable plutonium, and is unviable without large taxpayer subsidies. President [Gerald] Ford banned export of reprocessing technology and President [Jimmy] Carter stopped reprocessing in the U.S. as nuclear non-proliferation measures; while [President Ronald] Reagan lifted the ban, no commercial interest has pursued this expensive boondoggle, since it is not a profitable enterprise. Our current president [George W. Bush] apparently intends for taxpayers to pay for the relapse to reprocessing.

At the end of 2005, Congress awarded $50 million to the U.S. Department of Energy (DOE) with instructions to make a new waste-reprocessing plan. DOE was directed to hold a "competition" among possible "host" communities and the "winner" would get the new reprocessing site with a goal to open by 2010. The [President Barack] Obama administration has canceled this plan; however members of Congress are urgently promoting these options in 2009.

Reprocessing Destabilizes Waste

The fuel rods are taken out of the assemblies, chopped up and then dissolved in nitric acid. The resulting highly radioactive and caustic stew is then processed to remove the plutonium and the uranium, leaving the highly radioactive fission products in the liquid. While there are methods to attempt to restabilize this material, there has been a fundamental loss in the stability of the dry ceramic pellet in the metal clad fuel rod.

1. Reprocessing is not recycling. The formation of fission products in the fuel rods makes high-level waste fundamentally different from the uranium it came from. It is not possible to remake the original fuel again from high-level waste—thus it is not a cycle.

2. Reprocessing does not reduce radioactivity. No credible expert says reprocessing reduces total radioactivity; some less informed sources imply this. Reprocessing does [not change] the amount of radioactivity—except to smear it around a large surface area, thereby diluting it without any actual reduction of radioactivity.

3. Reprocessing does not reduce waste volume; to the contrary, fuel pellet volume is magnified by a factor of 100–100,000. The resulting "dilution" allows the reclassification from "high-level" to the so-called "low-level" waste category, which is still deadly.

The King Midas story of childhood teaches about the hazard of greed. Radioactive waste contaminates everything it comes in contact with—but instead of turning it all to gold, everything it comes in contact with is turned to expensive, dangerous radioactive waste!

A stated goal of reprocessing is to use plutonium for reactor fuel. The most common form is MOX (short for "mixed oxide"), made from plutonium and uranium-238 (depleted uranium). While today's reactors can use MOX fuel, it is both *riskier* and *more hazardous*: MOX is harder to control, and twice as deadly as uranium fuel if control is lost. MOX does not "solve" the waste problem since reprocessing MOX fuel is even harder than reprocessing uranium fuel, and not widely done. Princeton [University's] Dr. Frank Von Hippel likens MOX use to "kicking the can down the road"—not dealing with the waste problem at all.

North Korea and Iran are the most recent examples of countries ready to join the "nuclear weapons club."

Plutonium Destabilizes Our World

High-level nuclear waste contains so much lethal radioactivity that the plutonium inside the waste fuel rods is effectively safeguarded. Separating out the plutonium makes it available for weapons use. For the United States to reverse more than 30 years of policy against recovering civil plutonium also reverses the moral authority with which the U.S. calls on other nations to refrain from this activity. North Korea and Iran are the most recent examples of countries ready to join the "nuclear weapons club." Reprocessing is a direct contradiction [of] U.S. reprimands of these nations for nuclear proliferation. The clear intention during the Bush administration to return to full-scale production of new nuclear weapons added to this atomic hypocrisy.

Far from putting the atomic genie back in the bottle, reprocessing creates millions of gallons of highly radioactive, caustic, destabilized high-level waste that history shows will leak; be evaporated; residues put into glass that may, or may not, retain the radioactivity for even a generation; and now, under a new policy, be left forevermore on the reprocessing site, mixed only with grout [construction material] in a thin effort to keep it from contaminating soil, water, food and our bodies. This is NO SOLUTION.

4

Low-Level Radioactive Waste Recycling Is No Longer Harmful

Ken Kingery

Ken Kingery is a science and research writer for the University of Idaho.

A new process of handling nuclear waste promises a break-through in waste management. This method uses supercritical fluids to dissolve toxic metals and recover enriched uranium from the ashes of contaminated materials. In the future, super-critical fluids might be used to make waste management even safer and more efficient.

A new recycling plant will soon recover uranium from the ashes of radioactive garbage to be recycled back into nuclear fuel using an efficient, environmentally friendly technology inspired by decaffeinated coffee. The technique's future may even hold the key to recycling the most dangerous forms of radioactive waste.

Over the course of 20 years, Chien Wai, a University of Idaho chemistry professor, has developed a process that uses supercritical fluids to dissolve toxic metals. When coupled with a purifying process developed in partnership with Sydney Koegler [a University of Idaho alumnus and an engineer with nuclear industry leader AREVA], enriched uranium can be re-covered from the ashes of contaminated materials. On

Ken Kingery, "Radioactive Waste Recycling No Longer a Pain in the Ash," University of Idaho, August 20, 2008. Reproduced by permission of the author.

Wednesday, Aug. 20 [2008], representatives from the company and the university will sign an agreement to share the technologies and pave the way for the recycling plant's construction.

When the carbon dioxide's pressure is returned to normal, it becomes a gas and evaporates, leaving behind only the extracted metals.

"Radioactive waste is a big problem facing the United States and the entire world," said Wai. "We need new, innovative technology, and I think supercritical fluid is one such technology that will play an important role in the very near future."

Supercritical Fluids

A supercritical fluid—in this case carbon dioxide—is any substance raised to a temperature and pressure at which it exhibits properties of both a gas and a liquid. When supercritical, the substance can move directly into a solid like a gas and yet dissolve compounds like a liquid. For example, says Wai, supercritical carbon dioxide has directly dissolved and removed caffeine from whole coffee beans for decades.

When the carbon dioxide's pressure is returned to normal, it becomes a gas and evaporates, leaving behind only the extracted metals. No solvents required, no acids applied, and no organic waste left behind.

"That's why decaffeinated coffee tastes so good," said Wai, while chuckling at the beauty and simplicity of the process. "There is no solvent used, and so no solvent [is] left behind."

Because the technology is so simple, cost-effective, and environmentally friendly, AREVA is eager to test its first full-scale use on 32 tons of incinerator ash in Richland, Wash.

The existing plant in Richland fabricates fuel for commercial nuclear power plants from raw enriched uranium supplied by utility customers as uranium hexafluoride (UF_6). During normal operation, common items including filters, rags, paper wipes, and gloves become contaminated with uranium. The waste is burned to reduce its volume and increase its uranium content, making it easier to recover the uranium.

Valuable Garbage

Nearly 10 percent of the ash's weight is usable enriched uranium, worth about $900 dollars per pound on today's market. This means about $5 million dollars is currently sitting in the garbage waiting to be recovered. The process may even become the basis of the next generation of plants designed to recover useful materials from spent fuel.

"This agreement and technology is something Idaho should be very proud of," said Wai of the supercritical fluid technology transfer. "We have developed something special. And to me, that something is important to Idaho and to the U.S., particularly as we look for alternate energy sources in the future."

The new recycling plant is expected to be operational in 2009 and will take about a year to process AREVA's ash inventory. When finished, much of its operating time can be devoted to ash received from other sites.

The technology licensing agreement that will be signed by the university and AREVA will allow AREVA to use several of Wai's discoveries to extract the metals from the ash. AREVA provided funding and will gain rights to the University of Idaho's share of a joint University of Idaho and AREVA patent developed in cooperation with Wai over the past four years that further separates the enriched uranium from the extracted metals.

"This process has been extremely collaborative—it's one of those that you just love," said Gene Merrell, the university's chief technology transfer officer and assistant vice president for research. "It's going to be a great deal that will benefit the University of Idaho, AREVA and the entire world."

Dissolving and extracting any desired metal—possibly even radioactive material from high-level radioactive waste—simply requires finding a binding agent that works.

Joint Research Comes to Fruition

Technology transfer is a process common to research universities. Rights to patents are sold to companies, or used to create new start-up companies, and benefit all parties involved. Not only do the technology's profits benefit the university and future research, it allows the university to ensure its technology is being used in a useful and efficient way.

But for Wai, this technology transfer is only the beginning. He is now working to make the technology even more environmentally friendly and also to recycle different forms of radioactive waste.

The key to Wai's research is to find a soluble chemical compound to bind with the uranium. Because carbon dioxide cannot directly dissolve metals such as uranium, a binding agent called a ligand is introduced to the equation. Once the ligand is applied, the supercritical carbon dioxide flows through the waste, dissolving both the ligand and the metals bounded to it. Dissolving and extracting any desired metal—possibly even radioactive material from high-level radioactive waste—simply requires finding a binding agent that works. Wai predicts supercritical fluids will be used in the not-too-distant future to recycle even higher levels of radioactive waste.

"To me, accomplishing that is important to Idaho and to the United States, particularly as we look for alternate energy sources in the future." said Wai. "I believe nuclear energy will play a very large role, and that it can be done in a very environmentally safe and sustainable way."

5

Storage of Low-Level Nuclear Waste Must Be Addressed

Joseph DiCamillo

Joseph DiCamillo is the general counsel of Studsvik, Inc., a subsidiary of a Swedish firm providing nuclear technology and radiological services to the nuclear industry around the world.

In the future, because of regulatory and other issues, many hospitals and universities and power plants will have to store their low-level nuclear waste on-site, close to the public, raising the specter of spills and leaks while becoming possible terrorist targets. While nuclear energy is a way to overcome energy dependency, the government must support technologies that stabilize and minimize nuclear waste before it is disposed, create disposal sites that are safe, and relieve public institutions of the burden to store low-level waste.

The public has long been familiar with the problem of high-level radioactive waste disposal at Yucca Mountain. In the next 12 months [summer 2007 until summer 2008], the nation will face a second crisis, of disposal of low-level waste. Low-level waste is not the spent fuel itself, but rather many objects that have absorbed radiation, such as pipes, tools, resins, filters, medical tools, protective clothing, and whole sections from decommissioned nuclear power plants.

The scheduled closing of the disposal facility in Barnwell, South Carolina, in June 2008 will leave the majority of reac-

Joseph DiCamillo, "A Second Crisis in Radioactive Waste," *The American*, August 17, 2007. Reproduced with the permission of the American Enterprise Institute for Public Policy Research, Washington, D.C.

tors unable to dispose of certain low-level waste. Hospitals, universities, and research facilities will also be affected. For the lowest-level radioactive waste there will be only one privately owned disposal site [in Clive, Utah] available for the majority of the waste generated. ... The answer to this challenge is in part additional disposal sites—a difficult proposition since most states don't want to allow new sites to be built within their borders. We also must take steps to assure that existing sites are used optimally. The best technology should be encouraged, including volume reduction, waste stabilization, and best disposal site management techniques to conserve space.

A Time to Act

Until now, our system has silently but effectively dealt with the disposal of low-level nuclear waste. However the GAO [Government Accountability Office] reports that this system no longer meets the disposal requirement for the United States. The consequences may harm the $15 billion per year commercial nuclear power industry, which is on the verge of a renaissance. As general counsel of Studsvik, a leading company involved in using modern technology to efficiently and safely dispose of low-level waste, it is clear to me that the government must act now.

After 2008, hospitals, universities, and commercial nuclear power stations will need to store the most dangerous classes of low-level waste indefinitely, on-site, and closer to the public.

For the lowest-level radioactive waste there will be only one privately owned disposal site available for the majority of the waste generated.

In the 1980s, Congress enacted a program permitting formation of multi-state compacts to encourage creation of more low-level waste disposal sites. Commercial nuclear generators and state governments spent over $800 million attempting to open new sites. States have resisted creating such facilities within their borders. As a result of this failure and the huge price of entry (licensing, public opposition, etc.), no new low-level waste disposal sites have opened in almost 20 years. Only three active, designated disposal sites exist, with one new site in Texas in the permitting processes. One, in Richland, Washington, . . . accepts waste from [only] 11 Northwestern and Rocky Mountain states (notably, only *one* reactor is in operation in these states).

The second, in Barnwell, South Carolina, has for years been open to disposal of low-level waste, but starting in June 2008, the site will accept waste from only three states (containing just 12 of America's 104 operational reactors). A bill to keep Barnwell more accessible failed when the South Carolina legislature declined to act. While the federal government seems concerned, it has not made clear how it will respond under its limited emergency powers to keep the site open for out-of-compact waste.

The third site, a privately owned facility in Clive, Utah, after 2008 will be the last remaining one to accept commercially generated low-level waste from across the nation. However, in March [2007], Utah's governor signed an agreement with the owner of the site, capping the volume of the lowest class of low-level waste (Class A) that Clive will accept, and forbidding delivery of higher activity "Class B" and "Class C" waste. It is unlikely the governor will revisit his decision.

Dangerous Targets for Attacks

Taken together, the South Carolina and Utah actions mean that after 2008, nuclear generators in 36 states will have access to no permanent disposal facilities for Class B and C waste. As a result, hospitals, universities, and commercial nuclear power [stations] will need to store the most dangerous classes of low-level waste indefinitely, on-site, and closer to the public.

Worse yet, guarding these myriad small storage sites from terror attacks is more difficult than securing a few designated disposal facilities.

Further, the nation is on the verge of markedly increasing the volume of low-level waste it generates. This increase is largely due to the growing number of older reactors now going off-line, requiring dismantling of the reactor and decommissioning of the site. At the same time, the nation is considering building approximately 20 new nuclear power reactors, the first application for construction of a new reactor [since the 1970s] having been recently submitted to NRC [Nuclear Regulatory Commission].

We must face this looming second crisis in nuclear waste disposal because nuclear energy itself is a direct and positive answer to our national goal of energy independence. It is also a key component in meeting expected demands for electricity. Without support for and expansion of nuclear energy, neither of these challenges can be achieved. The Administration and Congress have recognized the key role that nuclear power will play in our future.

We must face this looming second crisis in nuclear waste disposal because nuclear energy itself is a direct and positive answer to our national goal of energy independence.

Nuclear energy has a proven safe record in electricity generation, and the technology is very inexpensive to operate compared to fossil fuels. As an example, South Carolina residents enjoy very low electricity rates in large part due to the significant portion of electricity generated by nuclear energy in that state.

Of no less importance is the fact that nuclear energy does not generate any greenhouse gases to create electricity. In the May 2005 edition of *Technology Review*, noted environmentalist Stewart Brand wrote: "The only technology ready to fill the gap and stop the carbon dioxide loading of the atmosphere is nuclear power."

Since it is clear that the 20-year-old system of state compacts has not led to sufficient waste disposal, national, state, and local governments must mobilize to help meet these challenges. Sound policy can address the looming crisis and provide the framework for the expansion of nuclear energy to safely and economically meet our Nation's energy demands.

Given these stakes, Congress, the Department of Energy, and the Nuclear Regulatory Commission must address this lack of disposal capacity. There are essentially three options.

First, the federal government could again try to encourage states to accept the waste. But [doing so] is unlikely to yield dividends, given that states have not welcomed radioactive waste from other states.

Second, the government could open up federally owned disposal sites to commercially generated low-level waste. This probably will not happen, because the federal government currently uses the three state sites to dispose of its own low-level waste.

A third option—the most environmentally conscientious one—is for the government to promote techniques that stabilize and minimize the volume of low-level waste prior to disposal. The Nuclear Regulatory Commission in 1981 issued a policy calling for increased attention to this option, but the Commission has done little to implement it. Those technologies can lengthen the life of disposal sites without the need for expansion, as well as substantially [reduce] the possibility of contamination outside of disposal site boundaries. An effective market-based option available to the federal government is to end the practice, followed by some disposal sites and state governments, of price discrimination. This practice results in the disposal facilities charging higher rates and taxes for stabilized and compacted waste than for the same volume of untreated waste. As a result, the United States fails to use optimally our scarce disposal capacity.

There is no more time to wait. The federal government must do everything possible to encourage or require the few existing disposal sites to stabilize and reduce the volume of low-level waste. And direct federal intervention is necessary to ensure that after June 2008, 28 states (housing 91 of the 104 reactors in the U.S.) can deposit their "Class B and C" waste in a designated disposal site, rather than leaving it scattered at power plants, universities, and hospitals. After the actions in Utah and South Carolina, the clock is ticking.

6

Nuclear Waste Storage Is the Best and Cleanest Option

Raymond J. Learsy

Raymond J. Learsy is the author of the updated version Over a Barrel: Breaking Oil's Grip on Our Future. *He is a member of the Woodrow Wilson International Center for Scholars.*

In order to reduce greenhouse gas emissions, nuclear energy should be expanded. While radioactive waste continues to be a problem, governments worldwide should look for safe deposits and new technologies that reduce waste and minimize its risk for the population. Countries that store waste could profit enormously, and instead of drilling for oil in Alaska, America should look into the possibility of storing nuclear waste.

The enveloping miasma [atmosphere that tends to deplete or corrupt] of climate change and its risk to us and future generations calls for dynamic action to forestall and hopefully prevent the disasters ahead.

It calls for a clear understanding that this is not a local, regional, national, continental, nor even hemispheric issue, but one that is fully global in its reach, its origins, and its ultimate impact. It will affect each and every one of us in some important way. And because of its universality, we cannot conquer the problem alone, though we can accomplish much through deed and example. Clearly, though, its global dimension demands a global response—and the time for meaningful cooperation on a world scale is slipping away.

Raymond J. Learsy, "Nuclear Waste: 'Not in My Backyard!' Then Whose?" *Huffington Post*, July 7, 2006. Reproduced by permission of the author.

Nuclear Power Has Potential

In my opinion—and some will disagree—the most effective and quickest way to reduce fossil fuel emissions, other than massively curtailing consumption, is to embrace the enormous potential of nuclear power. The question before us then is how to expedite the construction of nuclear facilities and get them up and running in the shortest time possible. Certainly, one of the major constraints is the storage and disposal of nuclear waste. This is not the only concern delaying nuclear power-plant construction, but it, more than any other, seems to be the elephant in the room that is holding back the broad and expeditious application of nuclear energy.

Concurrent to nuclear waste storage sites, we also need to develop advanced recycling technologies that do not produce separated plutonium. This would significantly diminish nuclear proliferation concerns, while recycling used fuel would dramatically reduce the amount of waste requiring permanent disposal.

Understandably, the cry of "not in my backyard"—even when the backyard is thousands of miles away at Nevada's Yucca Mountain—has been raised to a deafening level, drowning out reasoned arguments. And this scenario is being replicated in virtually every corner of the world where nuclear power is being contemplated or expanded.

The question before us ... is how to expedite the construction of nuclear facilities and get them up and running in the shortest time possible.

Yet France, where nearly 80 percent of that nation's electricity is generated by nuclear power (versus about 20 percent in this country, where the newest nuclear facility dates to the 1970s), finds no such objections. One has to wonder why the French, not otherwise celebrated for their quiet acquiescence [acceptance], accede to a set of conditions that, on their face, would have American communities up in arms.

The answer is not clear because, in large measure, the entire issue is shielded by a decree of "national security," which is meant to block debate. You see, France sends thousands of tons of nuclear waste to Russia each year. And though we know some details of the arrangement, much is still kept from public view. And that's a pity. France's arrangement just might provide the kernel of a solution to the global problem of nuclear waste. If the Franco-Russian program could be applied globally, it could offer a solution that transcends borders, is effective, environmentally rational, and secure.

Working out the details of agency oversight of nuclear waste depots would take some doing, but given the importance of the issue, it needs [to] be done.

Finding the Right Backyard

There are vast reaches of the world where nuclear waste disposal would have a truly minimal social impact and present the least possible environmental concern. Siberia, the Australian outback, ... the Gobi Desert, [and] the Canadian Shield among others, come to mind. Stretches of land that could provide an urgently needed "backyard" to allow the world to get on with the pressing need to expand the use of economical, carbon-free nuclear energy.

The International Atomic Energy Agency [IAEA], working under the auspices of the United Nations, already oversees the inspection and monitoring of nuclear power and fissionable materials around the world. The IAEA has, in its way, become the world watchdog on nuclear matters. Could the agency not also take on the oversight of international nuclear waste sites that would be accessible to all the world's nuclear power plants? The IAEA or some similar agency could be given full control over both storage and security at the sites. Admittedly, working out the details of agency oversight of nuclear waste depots would take some doing, but given the importance of the issue, it needs [to] be done.

Such a program could be very profitable for any country agreeing to undertake nuclear waste storage. The Russian government, for example, recently passed a law to allow additional storage of nuclear waste on Russian soil. The Ministry of Atomic Energy, or Minatom, claims that 10,000 to 20,000 tons of high-level nuclear waste could be imported over the next decade for storage and reprocessing, and it expects to earn $20 billion from the waste-storage business. Russia is considering two separate sites, Chelyabinsk-65 (for reprocessing) and the Novaya Zemlya archipelago in the Northern Arkhangelsk region (dust off your atlas).

Storage Can Be Profitable

Australia, with some 30 percent of the world's uranium reserves, is currently meeting 20 percent of the world's need. With nuclear expansion in China and India, this off-take will grow considerably in the years ahead. Business proposals aimed at Australia, which has ideal geological conditions for waste storage, are proliferating [increasing]. The Australian government is not unaware of these overtures, which promise to be highly profitable.

Now for a suggestion closer to home—and forgive me if I duck the slings and arrows that will be coming my way. Rather than drilling the Arctic National Wildlife Refuge [ANWR], with the wide and intrusive footprint ANWR oil development would entail, what if we set aside a very significantly smaller landmass as our own Novaya Zemlya archipelago to serve as a national depot for nuclear waste? We could then get on with building nuclear energy plants here at home and start taking a big bite out of our fossil fuel emissions. The caribou and polar bears would still have ample room to roam and happily carry on. And do not forget, they, too, have a vested interest in stopping and hopefully reversing global warming!

7

Underground Nuclear Waste Storage Is Not the Only Option

Matthew L. Wald

Matthew L. Wald is a reporter in the Washington bureau of the New York Times.

Since the funding for the central nuclear waste deposit site at Yucca Mountain has been cut, other options for nuclear waste disposal are needed. One solution is a mine outside Carlsbad, N.M., that contains rock salt that shows water trapped in crystals dating back 225 million years, suggesting that the salt would keep nuclear waste from being transported through the rock by water. Another solution is to store the dry-casks of spent nuclear fuel on-site for a longer period of time, which would give the waste more time to cool down and so reduce the number of long-term waste storage repositories required. A third possibility would be to use "fast reactors" to break up actinides (elements between actinium and lawrencium on the periodic table, including plutonium) with neutrons traveling at a higher speed, reducing both the volume and the half-life of the nuclear waste.

Two weeks after President Barack Obama pulled the plug on Yucca Mountain, the site near Las Vegas where the federal government has been trying for 22 years to open a repository for nuclear waste, geochemist James L. Conca came to Washington, D.C., with an idea in his pocket.

Matthew L. Wald, "What Now for Nuclear Waste?" *Scientific American*, August 2009, pp. 46–58. Copyright © 2009 by Scientific American, Inc. Reproduced by permission of the author.

Conca has been assigned by the state of New Mexico to monitor the environment around a different federal nuclear dump, one used for defense-related plutonium, and where others see problems, he sees opportunity.

The long battles over nuclear waste have produced much study and argument, epic legal wrangling and one mass-produced souvenir: a plastic bag labeled "Permian Age Rock Salt" that holds clear hunks of crystal mined from the Waste Isolation Pilot Plant 2,150 feet under the Chihuahuan Desert outside of Carlsbad, N.M. Conca, director of the Carlsbad Environmental Monitoring and Research Center at New Mexico State University, delights in giving away the little bags, telling recipients to hold the crystals up to the sunlight and peer through the translucent salt as if they were candling an egg.

Inside the chunks are little bubbles of water—what geologists call inclusions—that have been trapped for 225 million years, traces of a long-gone sea. They look a bit like bubbles trapped in Jell-O. Inclusions indicate how fast water, the vector for spreading waste, can move through the rock; in this case, Conca says, the timeline is encouraging. The salt naturally creeps in to close any cracks, so the water remains trapped. "Permeability is not just very low but zero," he says. When it comes to a place to put something that will be hazardous for a million years—the wastes that were to go to Yucca, for example—"you couldn't engineer something this good," he observes.

Conca's position is not shared by the elected leaders of New Mexico—if it were, the arguing would be over by now. But it is an indication that while the problem of nuclear waste remains unsolved, there are a number of reasonable candidate solutions. Some, like Carlsbad, resemble Yucca in kind if not location—find a quiet area and bury the stuff. Others rely on increasingly complex recycling schemes. But until elected officials implement an alternative plan—a process, if Yucca is any guide, that could take decades—the waste will languish at 131 storage sites around the country [*see box on page 52*].

The Collapse

This delay may not be an entirely bad thing. So far, at least, the interim waste being stored on-site at power plants is well inventoried and managed. It does not cascade from storage lagoons, as a billion gallons of toxic coal wastes did from a Tennessee Valley Authority power plant in December 2008. And unlike carbon dioxide, it does not disperse into the atmosphere to be counted in worrisome parts per million, an index of climate sickness akin to the white blood cell count of an infected patient. It does, however, accumulate and linger, in some cases longer than the reactor that produced it. The waste debate has gone on so long that there are now 10 "orphan" sites, radioactive mausoleums where the power plant is gone but the waste remains.

"Waste" might not be quite the right word; technically, the term for the bulk of the material to be buried is "spent nuclear fuel." The civilian stuff starts out as a fuel assembly—a bundle of thin-walled metal tubes, each filled with ceramic pellets of uranium oxide the size of pencil erasers. In the absence of free neutrons, this uranium is extremely stable. Power plant technicians handle the fresh fuel wearing nothing more than white gloves—and the gloves are for the protection of the fuel, not the workers.

After it arrives on site, the fuel is lowered into the outermost regions of a circular reactor vessel, which is sealed up and run for one to two years. Then the vessel is opened, the innermost, oldest fuel is removed, and the younger fuel moved toward the center. Usually a given fuel assembly will stay in the vessel for three cycles, which can last a total of anywhere from three to six years.

When a fuel assembly comes out, highly radioactive fission products such as strontium 90 and cesium 137 are generating tens of kilowatts of heat. If the assembly were cooled merely by air, the metal surrounding the nuclear material would melt; it might even burn. So the assemblies are kept submerged in a spent-fuel pool, a steel-lined concrete pool with water so clean that a drop of tap water would pollute it. These fission products burn hot but relatively quickly. Their half-life—the time it takes for half the material to transmute into more stable elements and release radiation—is measured in mere years. Heat production falls by 99 percent in the first year. It falls by another factor of five by the time the fuel is five years old and by another 40 percent by year 10.

After a few years the rods no longer need to be stored in water. They are transferred into steel sleeves, then drained, dried, pumped full of an inert gas and sealed. The sleeves are loaded into giant concrete casks and put into on-site storage near the reactor. Inside its concrete-and-steel silo, the fuel produces so little heat that it can be cooled by the natural circulation of air.

The long-term challenge is dealing with the actinides, materials created when uranium absorbs a neutron but refuses to split apart. These elements have half-lives in the hundreds of thousands of years. The Department of Energy originally set out to demonstrate that Yucca was safe for 10,000 years, yet it acknowledged that peak radiation releases would come after about 300,000 years. Opponents seized on that disparity, and in 2004 the U.S. Court of Appeals for the Federal Circuit ruled that the DOE had to demonstrate that the waste could be stored safely for one million years.

Yucca was never the leading candidate from a scientific point of view. A volcanic structure, it became the leading candidate when it was chosen in 1987 by the best geologists in the U.S. Senate. Before politicians stepped in, aiming to speed up the selection process and also to guarantee that the waste would not go anywhere else, Yucca was on a list of possible locations, along with sites in Texas and Washington State. The

DOE and its predecessor agency put these sites on the list for their scientific promise and partly for reasons of convenience—in the case of Yucca Mountain, the federal government already owned the place, and it was adjacent to a nuclear weapons test site.

Yucca fell out of the running for pretty much the same reason: politics. In 1987 the speaker of the House was a Texan, Jim Wright, and so was the vice president, George H. W. Bush. The House majority leader was Tom Foley of Washington State, and Harry Reid was a first-term senator from Nevada. Washington State and Texas dropped off the list. Now Reid is the majority leader, and the president won Nevada's four electoral votes partly by promising a new look at nuclear waste. The politics of geology has changed.

A purely scientific evaluation of competing geologies might find a better choice. "Salt is nice, in some senses, from a geologic perspective," says Allison M. Macfarlane, a geochemist and assistant professor of environmental science and policy at George Mason University and a frequently mentioned candidate for a vacant seat on the Nuclear Regulatory Commission. But if the salt is heated, the watery inclusions mobilize and flow toward the heat, she points out, so burying spent fuel there would require waiting until the hot waste products cool down a bit—somewhere around the second half of this century.

Macfarlane helped to organize a conference called "Toward a Plan B for U.S. High-Level Nuclear Waste Disposal" in July 2007, an event that mostly demonstrated that there was no plan B. The U.S. could find another solution, though, she says, if it used a more open, fair process for choosing sites—in other words, if it took the choice away from the politicians.

Plan B

It was never supposed to come to this. The Nuclear Waste Policy Act of 1982 specified that utilities had to pay into a government-administered Nuclear Waste Trust Fund a tenth of a cent for every kilowatt-hour of energy their reactors generated. The government, in turn, agreed to find a place to bury the waste. The DOE forced the utilities to sign contracts and promised to begin taking deliveries in January 1998.

Before President Obama submitted his 2010 budget, cutting funding for Yucca Mountain to a perfunctory $197 million, the official opening date was scheduled for 2017. And the department estimated that as of that date, it was liable for damages of $7 billion to the utilities, possibly the world's largest late fee. The price rises by $500 million every additional year of delay. If the science and engineering can come together, a fix is worth a lot of money.

Another possible solution revisits a decision made over three decades ago. By volume, about 95.6 percent of the spent fuel that comes out of a reactor is the same uranium oxide in the original fuel. The rest of the spent fuel is made of hot fission products (3.4 percent) and long-lived actinides such as plutonium (1 percent). At the start of the nuclear age, the plan was to recycle the uranium and plutonium into new fuel, discarding only the short-lived fission products. In theory, this would reduce the volume of waste by up to 90 percent. But President Gerald Ford banned recycling in 1976, and his successor, President Jimmy Carter, a former officer in the nuclear navy, concurred. The reason they gave was proliferation risk— the plutonium could also be used for bombs, so the reprocessing technology would be risky in Third World hands. (The economics have also been unfavorable.)

With the Ford decision, the U.S. committed itself to an "open" fuel cycle, meaning that the fuel would make a one-way trip—cradle to grave—as opposed to a "closed" cycle, where much of the fuel would have made a second or third pass through the reactor. It also made questions over waste a perennial part of the nuclear conversation. Various proposals have been floated over the years. Some have advocated shooting the stuff into space (a challenge, given its weight and the less-than-perfect success rate of launch vehicles). Others have suggested burying the waste at the borders of geologic plates and letting it slide over the eons back into the earth's mantle.

Instead it is filling up spent-fuel pools and then being shifted into dry casks, the steel-lined concrete silos. Although dry-cask storage might seem like a precarious and accidental solution, there is much to recommend it. Barring an accident such as dropping the sleeve on the racks of fuel in the pool, not much can go wrong. A terrorist attack could conceivably breach a cask, but the material inside is still a solid and is unlikely to go far. A terrorist group with a few rocket-propelled grenades and the talent to aim them well could find far more devastating targets than dry casks.

Storage space is also not an immediate concern. "There is enough capacity on our existing nuclear plants, if not for the rest of the century, then for a good portion of it," says Revis James, director of the Energy Technology Assessment Center at the Electric Power Research Institute, a utility consortium based in Palo Alto, Calif. "You could survive with aboveground storage for quite a while." Moreover, he says, "we're talking about a volume of waste that in the greater scheme of things is pretty small." (According to the International Atomic Energy Agency, a 1,000-megawatt reactor produces about 33 tons a year of spent fuel—enough to fill the bed of a large pickup truck.) As we face the threat of global warming, it would be a mistake to dismiss nuclear energy—an energy source that produces no green-house gases—on the basis of waste, he argues.

In addition, waste is a changing thing. The longer it is held in interim storage, the more material decays and the easier it is to deal with. While existing federal law sets the capacity of Yucca in terms of tons of waste, the real limit is heat. If the fuel is hot enough and packed closely enough to boil the groundwater, it will create steam that can fracture the rock, increasing the speed with which waste can eventually escape. The older the fuel, the lower the heat output and the smaller the repository required. (Or rather the smaller the *number* of repositories required—by 2017 the U.S. will already have accumulated far more nuclear waste than Yucca was legally supposed to take.)

As a result, dry-cask storage has shifted from its original role as a short-term solution to a viable medium-term solution. Existing reactors operate under a "waste confidence" doctrine, which says that while there is no repository now, there is "reasonable assurance" that there will be one by 2025. With that position now untenable, the Nuclear Regulatory Commission's staff has drafted new language, saying that the waste can be stored in casks for decades at reactors with no environmental effect, until burial is available. The change should make it easier to construct new reactors even in the absence of a long-term plan for the waste they will produce.

Not everyone is so sanguine. Arjun Makhijani, president of the antinuclear group Institute for Energy and Environmental Research, filed dissenting language with the commission earlier this year. He argued that it is irresponsible to assume that acceptable burial sites will one day become available. "A scientific explanation of the term 'reasonable assurance' requires either physical proof that such a [long-term storage] facility exists," he wrote, or firm evidence that one could be built using existing technology. Yet there is no validated model of any facility that proves that the waste is highly likely to stay isolated for hundreds of thousands of years, he says.

Others object to long-term storage on the surface. Certainly the nuclear power industry would like the government to put the waste underground, out of sight and out of mind. Keeping the stuff on the surface also means kicking the ball down the road for future generations. "I think it's a cop-out," Macfarlane says "I think we need to work toward a solution." Surface storage means institutional control, she says: "We have no guarantee what the government is going to be 100 years from now or if there's going to be one."

Accelerated Breakdown

There is another alternative: hurrying up the decay chain. Although nuclear recycling facilities of the kind rejected by the U.S. in the 1970s can recycle only the plutonium in spent fuel, plutonium is just one of a dozen or so long-lived actinides. A broader solution is industrial-grade transubstantiation: using a new kind of reactor to break down the actinides [see "Smarter Use of Nuclear Waste," by William H. Hannum, Gerald E. Marsh and George S. Stanford; *Scientific American*, December 2005].

General Electric is promoting a "fast reactor" that breaks up actinides with high-energy neutrons—the same subatomic particles that sustain the chain reactions in the current generation of reactors, only moving at a much higher speed. "It reduces volume on the order of 90 percent and cuts the half-life to less than 1,000 years instead of hundreds of thousands of years," says Lisa Price, GE Hitachi Global's senior vice president of nuclear fuel. "That can change the characteristics of what the long-term disposal site ultimately has to be." (The calculation assumes reuse of the recovered uranium, too—something that is very difficult in conventional reactors.)

But this solution requires one new fast reactor for every three or four now running to process the spent fuel, a tough challenge at a time when the industry is having trouble simply resuming construction of the kind of reactor it built 30 years ago. One of the main arguments against such reactors is cost—a fast reactor is cooled by molten sodium rather than water, and the advanced design is estimated to cost anywhere from $1 billion to $2 billion more per reactor than a similarly sized conventional reactor [see "Rethinking Nuclear Fuel Recycling," by Frank N. von Hippel; *Scientific American*, May

2008]. Democrats in Congress blocked most funding for fast reactors late in the Bush administration, and President Obama does not favor them.

Finally, Yucca could always come back. "Thirty-nine states have high-level waste—either civilian spent nuclear fuel or Navy spent nuclear fuel or defense program high-level waste," says Edward F. Sproat III, who was the DOE official in charge of the Yucca project for the last two and a half years of the Bush administration. The waste is "all destined to go to Yucca, and there's no other place to send it." He and others argue that President Obama and Senator Reid have the political power to block funding but not to change the 1987 amendment to the Nuclear Waste Policy Act that targets Yucca exclusively. And if Congress debates where else to put it, he says, "everybody knows their state is going to be back in play."

8

The Private Sector Should Manage Nuclear Waste

Jack Spencer

Jack Spencer is the Research Fellow in Nuclear Energy at The Heritage Foundation's Roe Institute for Economic Policy Studies.

Despite the Nuclear Waste Policy Act, the government has not taken responsibility for accumulating nuclear waste, further hindering an efficient nuclear policy. Instead of merely disposing of all nuclear waste, depleted fuel should be recycled. Since the government has proved slow and inefficient in handling the problem, the private sector should become responsible for nuclear waste management. Yucca Mountain should be used as a deposit beyond the irrational restrictions set by the government, and new repositories should be explored. Only the private sector can lead the way out of the nuclear waste impasse and make America a leader in nuclear energy.

The Nuclear Waste Policy Act of 1982 attempted to establish a comprehensive disposal strategy for high-level nuclear waste. This strategy has failed. The government has spent billions of dollars without opening a repository, has yet to receive any waste, and is amassing billions of dollars of liability. Furthermore, the strategy has removed any incentive to find more workable alternatives. For those that actually produce waste and would benefit most from its efficient disposal, this strategy has created a disincentive for developing sustainable, market-based waste-management strategies.

Jack Spencer, "A Free-Market Approach to Managing Used Nuclear Fuel, Backgrounder #2149," *Heritage Foundation*, June 23, 2008. Copyright © 2008 *The Heritage Foundation*. Reproduced by permission.

The strategy codified in the Nuclear Waste Policy Act seemed straightforward and economically sound when it was developed in the early 1980s. It charged the federal government with disposing of used nuclear fuel and created a structure through which users of nuclear energy would pay a set fee for the service—a fee that has never been adjusted, even for inflation. These payments would go to the Nuclear Waste Fund, which the federal government could access through congressional appropriations to pay for disposal activities.

The federal government has accumulated approximately $27 billion (fees plus interest) in the Nuclear Waste Fund and has spent about $8 billion to prepare the repository for operations, leaving a balance of around $19 billion. Utility payments into the fund total about $750 million annually. Yet the repository has never opened, despite the expenditure of billions of dollars.

The United States has 58,000 tons of high-level nuclear waste stored at more than 100 sites in 39 states.

The taxpayers have fared no better. The Nuclear Waste Policy Act set January 31, 1998, as the deadline for the federal government to begin receiving used fuel. The government's refusal to take possession of the used fuel has made both the federal government and the taxpayers liable to the nuclear power plant operators for an increasingly enormous amount that is projected to reach $7 billion by 2017.

The federal government's inability to fulfill its legal obligations under the 1982 act has often been cited as a significant obstacle to building additional nuclear power plants. Given nuclear power's potential to help solve many of the nation's energy problems, now is the time to break the impasse over managing the nation's used nuclear fuel.

The Current Irrational System

The United States has 58,000 tons of high-level nuclear waste stored at more than 100 sites in 39 states, and its 104 commercial nuclear reactors produce approximately 2,000 tons of used fuel every year. The Yucca Mountain repository's capacity is statutorily limited to 70,000 tons of waste (not to mention the problems associated with even opening the repository). Of this, 63,000 tons will be allocated to commercial waste, and 7,000 tons will be allocated to the Department of Energy (DOE).

These are arbitrary limitations that Congress set without regard to Yucca's actual capacity. As currently defined by the Nuclear Waste Policy Act, Yucca would reach capacity in about three years unless the law is changed. Thus, even if Yucca becomes operational, it will not be a permanent solution, and the nation would soon be back at the drawing board.

The repository's actual capacity, however, is much larger than the current limit. Congress should repeal the 70,000-ton limitation immediately and instead let technology, science, and physical capacity determine the limit. Recent studies have found that the Yucca repository could safely hold 120,000 tons of waste. According to the DOE, that should be enough to hold all of the used fuel produced by currently operating reactors. Some believe the capacity is even greater.

Yet even with an expanded capacity of 120,000 tons, Yucca Mountain could hold only a few more years of America's nuclear waste if the U.S. significantly increases its nuclear power production. According to one analysis, America's current operating reactors would generate enough used fuel to fill a 70,000-ton Yucca right away and a 120,000-ton Yucca over their lifetime. If nuclear power production increased by 1.8 percent annually after 2010, a 120,000-ton Yucca would be full by 2030. At that growth rate, without recycling any used fuel, the U.S. would need nine Yucca Mountains by the turn of the century.

Given the difficulty of opening one repository, relying on future repositories would be extremely risky. With the right mix of technologies such as storage and recycling, Yucca could last almost indefinitely.

Many technologies exist to recover and recycle different parts of the used fuel.

Using Resources More Wisely by Recycling

The current U.S. policy is to dispose of all used fuel by moving it directly from the reactors into Yucca Mountain for permanent storage without any additional processing. This is a monumental waste of resources. To generate power, reactor fuel must contain 3 percent to 5 percent enriched fissionable [having the capacity to be split atomically] uranium (uranium-235). Once the enriched uranium falls below that level, the fuel must be replaced. Yet this "used" fuel generally retains about 95 percent of its fissionable uranium, and that uranium, along with other byproducts in the used fuel, can be recovered and recycled. Regrettably, the current system's structure provides no incentive for the private sector to pursue this option.

Many technologies exist to recover and recycle different parts of the used fuel. The French have been the most successful in commercializing such a process. They remove the uranium and plutonium and fabricate new fuel. Using this method, America's 58,000 tons of used fuel contain roughly enough energy to power every household in America for 12 years.

Other technologies show even more promise. Indeed, most of them, including the process used in France, were developed originally in the United States. Some recycling technologies would leave almost no waste at all and would lead to the recovery of an almost endless source of fuel, but none of these processes has been commercialized successfully in the United States, and this will take time. Until the future of nuclear power in the U.S. becomes clearer, it will be impossible to know which technologies will be most appropriate to pursue in this market.

Ultimately, the private sector should make these decisions. Valuing used fuel against the costs of permanent burial is a calculation best done by companies that provide fuel-management services.

Overhauling Used-Fuel Management in the U.S.

The success of a sustained rebirth of nuclear energy in the U.S. depends largely on disposing of nuclear waste safely. New nuclear plants could last as long as 80 years, but to reap the benefits of such an investment, a plant must be able to operate during that time. Having a practical pathway for waste disposal is one way to ensure long-term plant operations. Establishing such a pathway would also mitigate much of the risk associated with nuclear power, but as long as the federal government is responsible for disposing of waste, it is the only entity with any incentive to introduce these technologies and practices.

The problem is that the federal government has never been able to fulfill its current waste disposal obligations, much less introduce new and innovative methods of waste management. Although the Department of Energy under its current leadership [George W. Bush] has opened the door to reform, that leadership will soon be replaced when the new President [Barack Obama] appoints his own team. Administrations come and go, but inflexible rules and bureaucracies that oversee waste management seem to endure forever, making it impossible for the government to respond effectively to a rapidly changing industry. When it does attempt to respond, it often acts in ways that make no business sense and are inconsistent with the actual state of the industry.

Many of these efforts culminate in large government programs. While some of these programs have some near-term benefit insofar as they demonstrate political support for nuclear power, encourage private and public research and development, and develop the nuclear industry, they inevitably do more harm than good. They are run inefficiently, are often never completed, cost the taxpayers billions of dollars, and are often not economically rational. Furthermore, they often forgo long-term planning, and this leads to unsustainable programs that ultimately set industry back by providing fodder for antinuclear critics and discouraging progress in the private sector.

Having a practical pathway for waste disposal is one way to ensure long-term plant operations.

A New Approach

Introducing market forces into the process and empowering the private sector to manage nuclear waste can solve the problem, but this will require major reform. The federal government will need to step aside and allow the private sector to assume the responsibility for managing used fuel, and the private sector should welcome that responsibility.

The primary goal of any strategy for used-fuel management should be to provide a disposition pathway for all of America's nuclear waste. The basic problem with the current system is that every nuclear power plant needs a place to put its waste, and Yucca Mountain is simply not big enough to hold it all under the current used-fuel management regime.

In other words, permanent geologic storage capacity is a finite resource on which the industry depends. If used-fuel management were a market-based system, this storage capacity would carry a very high value. A new system should price geologic storage as a finite resource and fold any costs into a fee for emplacing nuclear waste in Yucca Mountain.

Repealing the Mil

The key to this new approach will be to transform how waste management is financed. Once market-based pricing is in place, the fee that nuclear energy consumers pay to the federal government for waste management should be repealed. Under the current system, consumers pay for waste disposition through a flat fee, called the mil, that is paid to the federal government at the rate of 0.1 cents per kilowatt-hour of nuclear-generated electricity. This fee as currently assessed has no market rationale. It is simply a flat fee that rate payers pay to the federal government. It has never been changed, not even for inflation.

In a market-based system, instead of paying a pre-set fee to the federal government to manage used fuel, nuclear power operators would fold waste-management costs into the operating cost, which would be reflected in the price of power. This cost might be higher or lower than the current fee; more important, it would reflect the true costs of nuclear power.

Pricing Geologic Storage as a Scarce Resource

The idea would be to price the space available in Yucca Mountain according to a set of relevant variables, including heat content of the waste, predicted production of used fuel, repository capacity, and lifetime operation costs. Each of these variables would help to determine the price of placing a given volume of waste in Yucca at any specific time.

As the repository is filled, the fee to emplace additional fuel would obviously increase. The fee could also increase, depending on the formula, as new plants are constructed or old plants' licenses are renewed because they would produce additional used fuel, thereby increasing the demand for repository space. Prices would be lower for waste that radiates less heat. Prices would fall if Yucca's capacity is expanded or if waste is reduced through alternative processes.

This would create a market for repository space. The fee could be structured in a number of ways. One example would be to charge a floating fee according to a predetermined formula. Under this scenario, the fee would shift constantly as the price variables change. For example, a volume of waste with less heat content would cost less to emplace than a similar amount with a higher heat profile. An alternative to a floating fee might be one that resets at timed intervals, such as once a year.

The exact structure and implementation of the fee could be determined at some future point. One simple option would be to divide the capacity available in Yucca by the lifetime costs to give a price to emplace an amount (e.g., a ton) of waste in the repository. As the repository was filled, the price per ton would increase.

Nuclear power operators could then decide, given the price to place waste in Yucca, how to manage their used fuel. As the price to access Yucca goes up, so will the incentive for nuclear operators to do something else with their used fuel. This should give rise to a market-based industry that manages used fuel in the U.S.

If a global nuclear renaissance does unfold, the prices for uranium and fuel services will likely rise.

A Market-Regulated System

The market would dictate the options available. Some operators may choose to keep their used fuel on site to allow its heat load to dissipate, thus reducing the cost of placing that waste into Yucca. Companies may emerge to provide interim storage services that would achieve a similar purpose. The operators could choose options based on their particular circumstances.

As prices change and business models emerge, firms that recycle used fuel would likely be established. Multiple factors would feed into the economics of recycling nuclear fuel. Operators would make decisions based not only on the cost of placing waste in Yucca, but also on the price of fuel.

If a global nuclear renaissance does unfold, the prices for uranium and fuel services will likely rise. This would place greater value on the fuel resources that could be recovered from used fuel, thus affecting the overall economics of recycling. Instead of the federal government deciding what to build, when to build it, and which technology should emerge, the private sector would make those determinations.

Some nuclear operators may determine that one type of recycling works for them, while others may decide that a different method is more appropriate. This would create competition and encourage the development of the most appropriate technologies for the American market.

Such a market for repository space could give rise to a broader market for geologic storage. As waste production causes Yucca storage costs to rise, companies could emerge that provide additional geologic storage at a lower price. This additional space would in turn reduce the value of the space available in Yucca.

Finding New Locations

Alternatively, as Yucca fills, nuclear operators may decide to develop additional geologic storage facilities in a joint venture. While this may seem unlikely, given the problems associated with opening Yucca Mountain, other communities may be more receptive to hosting a repository once a reliable safety record is established and the economic benefits of hosting a repository are demonstrated. The federal government would still take title to any waste placed in future repositories once they are decommissioned.

Predicting how a market might evolve is impossible, but unlike the government-run process that led to the Yucca Mountain site—a process mired in politics—private entities would establish the path forward by working with government regulators. Private entities would also be able to pursue their plans without having to contend with as much of the bureaucratic inertia that accompanies government-run operations.

Most important, this system would encourage the introduction of new technologies and services into the market as they are needed, as opposed to relying on the federal government. New technologies would not be hamstrung by red tape or overregulation. This system would also allow for the possibility of no expansion of nuclear power. If the U.S. does not expand nuclear power broadly, there is probably no reason to build recycling or interim storage facilities.

Establishing a Private Organization to Manage Yucca Mountain

As permanent geologic storage is commoditized, the problem then becomes one of establishing responsibility for managing that scarce resource. Leaving that responsibility with the government provides no benefits. No overarching need mandates that the government must manage Yucca Mountain or used nuclear fuel. Furthermore, leaving this responsibility in the hands of government comes with all kinds of pitfalls, including inflexibility, inefficiency, politics, and being subject to annual appropriations, to name a few. Similarly, a public-private partnership is not necessary and has no inherent advantages.

Instead, a completely new organization—a private entity (PE)—should be established to manage Yucca Mountain. The PE's purpose would be to ensure that Yucca is available to support the commercial nuclear industry's need for permanent geologic storage indefinitely and to set the fee for placing waste in Yucca. This fee would be the primary mechanism for managing access to the repository. Its one operating mandate should be to remain open to receive waste either until a second repository is opened or until the last commercial nuclear power plant ceases operations.

The federal government should not be part of the management team. The PE could be organized in any number of ways. It could take the form of a nonprofit organization that is independent of but represents the nation's nuclear energy producers. Such a structure would ensure that no operator receives preferential treatment and that the PE operates as a service to all nuclear operators. It also would prevent a profit-seeking entity from holding a monopoly over a key asset on which an entire industry depends. The federal government would provide oversight through the Nuclear Regulatory Commission (NRC) and other appropriate agencies.

The PE should be created as soon as possible and immediately commence a three-year transition plan, which would coincide with the NRC's review of the Department of Energy's application for a Yucca Mountain construction permit. During the transition period, the PE would work with the Department of Energy's Office of Civilian Radioactive Waste Management to move the application for the Yucca construction permit through the NRC. After three years, when the license is granted, the PE would take control of Yucca operations, which would include overseeing Yucca construction and preparing for long-term operations.

The current approach to managing used nuclear fuel is systemically broken.

Establishing a Waste Disposal Fund

The NRC requires that each nuclear plant operator establish a funding mechanism to ensure that resources will be available to decommission the plant once operations cease. This is achieved either through guarantees from its parent company or by establishing a decommissioning fund. This protects the taxpayer from the financial obligations of plant decommissioning if the operator becomes financially unable to carry out that responsibility.

A similar funding mechanism should be required for new plant licenses and life extensions to cover the costs of waste disposal once the mil is repealed. This could be included in the decommissioning fund or set up as a separate entity. It would not be a payment to the federal government and would always be controlled by the nuclear operator. The monies set aside should be adequate to finance the geologic disposal of any used fuel held on-site in dry storage. This guarantees that waste disposal funds will be available, even if the operator becomes insolvent. . . .

A Time to Act

The current approach to managing used nuclear fuel is systematically broken. It was developed to support a nuclear industry that was largely believed to be in decline; that is no longer the case. The federal government promised to take title of the used fuel and dispose of it; this removed any incentive for the private sector to develop better ways to manage the fuel that could be more consistent with an emerging nuclear industry. And the federal government has proven incapable of fulfilling its obligations to dispose of the fuel.

The current system is driven by government programs and politics. There is little connection between used-fuel management programs and the needs of the nuclear industry. Any successful plan must grow out of the private sector. The time has come for the federal government to step aside and allow utilities, nuclear technology companies, and consumers to manage used nuclear fuel.

Overhauling the nation's nuclear-waste management regime will not be easy. It will require a significant amendment of the Nuclear Waste Policy Act and a long-term commitment by Congress, the [presidential] Administration, and industry. But developing such a system would put the United States well on its way to reestablishing itself as a global leader in nuclear energy.

9

Genetic Engineering Could Help Reduce Toxic Waste

Katharine Mieszkowski

Katharine Mieszkowski is a senior writer for Salon.com.

Accelerated bioremediation and genetic engineering might help scientists find ways to decontaminate toxic waste. By speeding up the natural process in the lab, bacteria can evolve more quickly and efficiently and help clean up the environment. Reducing pollution has been an elusive goal, but genetic engineering might help to reduce the effects of global warming.

Erin Brockovich used the law to take on toxic waste. Today, she'd want a microbiologist in her corner, too.

Using bacteria and plants to neutralize contaminants [toxic particles and materials] in polluted areas is a decades-old practice known as "bioremediation." But naturally occurring organisms can't mop up all our toxic messes. Evolution simply hasn't had enough millennia to produce organisms that can effectively decontaminate all the waste dished out by chemical, oil and nuclear weapons production facilities. Many contaminated sites contain multiple toxins, so while an organism may be able to stomach one, another kills it off. Oil spills, like the many that Hurricane Katrina caused, might require dozens of enzymes to fully degrade.

Katharine Miezkowski, "The Big Idea: Accelerated Bioremediation," *Salon.com*, October 21, 2005. Copyright © 2005 *Salon.com*. This article first appeared in *Salon.com*, at http://www.salon.com. An online version remains in the Salon archives. Reprinted with permission.

Speeding up Evolution

Enter "accelerated bioremediation" and genetic engineering, which scientists such as Dr. David Ackerley of Stanford University's Matin Laboratory are using to speed up evolution in the lab—turning living organisms into better toxic-fighting machines. In one dream scenario, an organism feeds off the toxic sludge in a Superfund site, then disappears when its cleanup work is done.

Of course, some critics have raised concerns that genetically modified organisms could have myriad unintended effects. But their release into the environment is tightly regulated by the Environmental Protection Agency, and the government has a big vested interest in getting it right. The U.S. Department of Energy funds labs like the one at Stanford where Ackerley works, through its Natural and Accelerated Bioremediation Research program, with the hopes of using their breakthroughs to clean up its own contaminated sites.

Ackerley, who will be continuing his research at Victoria University of Wellington in New Zealand next year [2006], told Salon how microbiologists are speeding up evolution in the lab to take on toxic waste.

Katharine Miezkowski: *Why do we need genetic engineering to help clean up contaminated sites?*

David Ackerley: The whole industrial revolution, the Cold War and the arms race, particularly nuclear weapons production, produced a huge number of massively contaminated sites, in particular heavy-metal contamination. What you're seeing for the first time in the history of the planet are compounds that would not arrive in nature. So there has never been any natural selection for bacteria to evolve a way of detoxifying these compounds.

We're trying to find ways of evolving enzymes to actually reduce and degrade these compounds. Our lab uses a set of techniques called "directed evolution" to try to mimic evolution in a test tube. We're asking: What would have happened if there had been this selective pressure, either on bacteria or on individual molecules? How would they have adapted to actually confront this problem?

What's an example that you're working on?

In our lab, we work on hexavalent chromium, which you might remember being the toxic nasty in the Erin Brockovich case. In that case, PG&E [Pacific Gas and Electric Company] was using chromate as a rust inhibitor in their cooling towers. They were dumping it in unlined pools, and it's incredibly soluble. So even though it was a couple of miles away from this little township, it was able to leach its way through subterranean waterways into the township's water supply.

The natural form of chromium in the environment is chromium-3. But the toxic form is chromium-6, and that's the form that is generated by a wide range of industries, including nuclear weapons production.

A lot of positive changes will be lost throughout evolution.

How do you take it on?

We broke down bacteria, and all of its constituent proteins, to try to find one protein—an enzyme—that was able to turn chromium-6 into chromium-3. We actually found one of these enzymes. What we're doing now is introducing a whole range of mutations into this enzyme, so basically just mimicking what would have happened through evolution. We've taken it out of the whole living cell, which is a really complicated system, and put just this one enzyme into the test tube, focusing on its ability to reduce chromate.

Normally when you have a selective pressure in evolution, it gets complicated by the fact that you have millions of other proteins and genes floating around inside the cell. So if you improve one quality, a lot of the time it's not going to make enough difference. A lot of positive changes will be lost throughout evolution. But here in a test tube we're focusing on just one gene, one protein and one activity. So, you have a lot more ability to select for the things that you really want. The simple view of evolution is that it happens through mutation in individual genes. So, you're basically accelerating the rate of evolution.

What are some of the toxins that biotechnologists are trying to engineer new approaches to now?

Some of the toxins that are being worked on are associated largely with nuclear weapons production, and these heavy metals like chromium and uranium. A lot of times what you're looking at is containing these compounds, because they can be highly soluble and they can spread through soil and waterways. So, if you can at least make them insoluble and contain them, you've won a large part of the battle.

Another common problem is arsenic, which is used in the tanning and timber industries. Then, there are a whole pile of these things like dioxins or polyaromatic hydrocarbons, which are produced through a huge range of industries, like coal and oil.

We're trying to play catch-up for our previous lack of understanding over the last 50 years.

Why is this field growing right now?

For a long time, people thought that with nuclear waste it was fine to just dig a big hole in the ground and dump it in. But now people are realizing that the subterranean environment is a very dynamic environment. Just because you've covered something up, and you can't see it anymore, doesn't mean that it doesn't have a way of spreading and causing massive environmental damage. I guess we're trying to play catch-up for our previous lack of understanding over the last 50 years.

I have friends in Greenpeace who really can't make up their mind whether I'm a good person or a bad person, because I'm trying to clean up the environment, but I'm doing it with genetic engineering.

10

Toxic Waste Trade Comes with Many Dangers

Beau Baconguis

Beau Baconguis is a campaign manager of Greenpeace Southeast Asia.

The Basel Convention seeks to restrict the trade of toxic waste, yet still, industrial nations such as Japan ship their waste to developing nations such as the Philippines, to be dumped without sufficient safety measures. Only the Basel Ban Amendment can help stop this dangerous trade, and the Philippines must look beyond short-term gains to protect their country from irreparable ecological damage.

When Sen. [of the Philippines] Miriam Defensor-Santiago gave her sponsorship speech in support of the Senate's ratification of the Japan-Philippines Economic Partnership Agreement (Jpepa), she branded the issue of toxic wastes "disruptive" and a "nonissue." She argued that signing on to the Basel Convention [an international convention to control the movement and disposal of hazardous waste] and having national laws such as RA 6969 [a 1990 act to control toxic substances and nuclear wastes] and other waste laws give the Philippines enough protection from toxic-waste dumping by Japan. Senator Santiago further stated that the Exchange of Notes signed by then Japanese Foreign Minister Taro Aso and [Philippines] Foreign Secretary Alberto Romulo also gives Filipinos the assurance that Japan will not export its toxic wastes to the country.

Beau Baconguis, Greenpeace Southeast Asia, "Toxics Not a 'Nonissue' in Jpepa," *Business Mirror*, August 15 & 16, 2008. Reproduced by permission of the author.

The senator is either missing the point or, more probably, deliberately attempting to cover up one of the strongest arguments against the trade pact. Toxic waste remains a major issue in the Jpepa—and alarming provisions within the agreement itself make toxic-waste trade from Japan to the Philippines not only possible, but also desirable.

A Dangerous Loophole

It would be worthwhile to note that although the Philippines and Japan . . . both signed on to the Basel Convention many years ago, Japan continues to send toxic waste to the Philippines. The intent of the Basel Convention is to prevent developed countries like Japan from dumping toxic wastes in developing countries. But the fact is, Japan is still sending its waste to the Philippines and other poorer neighbors. The Basel Convention, no matter the good intent, has a loophole—exports that are toxic may be allowed with prior notification and consent of the importing country, and if the material is deemed to have commercial value or is declared recyclable.

This gap has been readily exploited by Japan, whose own waste dumps are now overflowing. In 1999, Japan shipped 122 containers of used diapers and medical and municipal wastes to the Philippines and declared these as "recyclable paper." The illegal shipment would not have been discovered if not for the unbearable stench coming from the containers. But despite that scandal, the Department of Environment and Natural Resources (DENR) continues to allow the entry of toxic materials, including electronic scraps, printed circuit boards, printed wiring boards, lead acid batteries and other toxic chemicals, again, for recycling. In 2003, the DENR listed used televisions, regenerated automotive batteries, electronic assemblies and scrap and scrap aluminum metal as some of our toxic-waste imports from Japan. Indeed, the Japan External Trade Organization (Jetro) recognizes the Philippines as "an active importer and exporter of waste and used products containing hazardous substances under its pre-notification and approval regulations." In short, Japan and the Philippines—both proud to be recognized as signatories to the Basel Convention—are clearly willing parties to the sort of shameful waste trade that the Convention rightfully seeks to prohibit. With Jpepa, the situation will become unimaginably worse: zero-tariff provisions on toxic and nuclear wastes will usher in unprecedented amounts of waste shipments into the Philippines.

> The intent of the Basel Convention is to prevent developed countries like Japan from dumping toxic wastes in developing countries.

A Flawed Agreement

The Toxic Substances and Hazardous and Nuclear Wastes Control Act (RA 6969), the Philippines' response to implement the Basel Convention, also carries the same loopholes of pre-notification and recycling. Therefore, even the issuance of Chemical Control Orders (CCOs) for asbestos, cyanide, mercury, ozone-depleting substances and polychlorinated biphenyls (PCBs), which have RA 6969 as their mother law, will not help protect the country from toxic dumping because the flaws of the Convention and the Act are carried through to the CCOs.

It is on the basis of these arguments that environment groups contend that the Exchange of Diplomatic Notes between the two countries does not present a way forward on the issue of toxic dumping. This side agreement says "Japan will not send, would not be exporting toxic wastes to the Philippines, as defined and prohibited under the laws of the Philippines and Japan, in accordance with the Basel Convention."

Perhaps one good thing that emerged from the Jpepa discussions is that the government is now finally realizing the importance of the Basel Ban Amendment. Senator Santiago ended her speech with calls for its ratification. This important amendment to the Basel Convention is meant to plug the recycling and pre-notification loopholes in the Convention to completely stem the movement of toxic wastes from developed to developing countries.

The Disgraceful Trade Must Stop

But unless the Executive branch transmits the amendment to the Senate, Senator Santiago's call is hollow. Officials of the DENR have themselves declared, in public, that they are not for the Basel Ban Amendment. It is, therefore, up to the Senate to ensure that this important safeguard is ratified. If the Senate disregards the Basel Ban Amendment—an international treaty meant to protect defenseless countries from toxic-waste trade—in the face of the imminent approval of the Jpepa—which legalizes and even makes lucrative such disgraceful trade—then our country will have truly reached the pits of indignity.

In the words of Okechukwu Ibeanu, special rapporteur [an investigator appointed by a deliberative body] of the Human Rights Council during the Basel Convention Conference of Parties 9 in Bali, Indonesia, in June [2008]: "Many developing countries, despite sometimes knowing the dangers of the waste, continue to accept hazardous products and toxic waste due to poverty and the quest for development. Is it worth the short-term monetary gain? Is it worth people falling sick [. . .] precious water sources contaminated permanently? I believe that we need to think of a better solution to generate income and development." . . .

[Filipino] senators must look beyond the short-term gains of the Jpepa, oppose the ratification of the treaty and vote in favor of a cleaner, toxic-free future for Filipinos.

11

Toxic Waste Leads to Environmental Racism

Heather Knight

Heather Knight is a San Francisco Chronicle *staff writer.*

Much of San Francisco's toxic waste has been dumped in poor, mostly minority-populated areas of the city. The residents don't have the financial means or the political clout to hire lawyers and bring about change, and many suffer severe medical conditions due to the exposure to toxins. The question of where and how to dispose of toxic waste has led to environmental racism, targeting underprivileged segments of society. Since these residents have no means to fight back, the waste is often improperly managed, leading to even worse health conditions.

When it comes to walking tours of San Francisco, energetic tourists can choose among dozens. They can take a literary tour of North Beach, stroll past the famous Victorian mansions on Alamo Square, view murals in the Mission or wander through the colorful alleys of Chinatown.

But one walking tour is different. It's in Hunters Point, a part of town largely ignored by publishers of tourist guides. And it's not centered on art, architecture or food. It's all about the pollutants and chemicals that contribute to what local public health authorities consider a neighborhood health crisis of major proportion.

Heather Knight, "Trudging on the Toxic Tour," *San Francisco Chronicle*, November 28, 2006. Copyright © 2006 Hearst Communications Inc., Hearst Newspaper Division. Reproduced by permission.

The Toxic Tour

It's the Toxic Tour—and if it doesn't sound like fun, that's the point. It's intended to show participants—mostly school groups—what happens when a largely poor, minority population lives on a swath of land containing 325 toxic sites.

"It's an equation that doesn't start to make that much sense health-wise," explained Rachel Pomerantz, 29, who leads the tours on behalf of the Hunters Point nonprofit Literacy for Environmental Justice.

On a recent morning, she huddled in the fog just outside the Hunters Point Shipyard with a group of teenagers from Downtown High.

She told them that more than 90 percent of residents of the broader Bayview-Hunters Point neighborhood are minorities and that many of them live in poverty. She added that the neighborhood's residents, who make up about 5 percent of San Francisco's population, contend with a third of the city's industry and 30 percent of its hazardous waste sites.

Environmental Racism

"Is that a coincidence?" she asked them. "Have you guys ever heard of the term 'environmental racism' before?"

"Does that still go on?" a boy asked her.

"What do you think?" she responded.

Eighty percent of San Francisco's sewage is treated in the neighborhood at a plant built in 1952 and expanded several times since then.

Though claims of environmental racism are controversial and debatable, a recent report by the city's Department of Public Health cites it—along with other factors such as social isolation and a lack of healthy food—as partly to blame for the bleak public health picture of those living in the neighborhood.

According to the report released in September [2006], residents of the poor, often violent part of the city are hospitalized for just about every disease—including asthma, diabetes and congestive heart failure—more than residents of any other neighborhood in the city.

A big reason, according to the document, is the area's hazardous environmental conditions. Eighty percent of San Francisco's sewage is treated in the neighborhood at a plant built in 1952 and expanded several times since then. Cement production and diesel bus storage also are prominent. Major freeways cut through the area, making vehicle pollution another concern.

Two stops on the Toxic Tour considered the worst offenders are the Hunters Point Shipyard and the power plant. The latter, run by PG&E [Pacific Gas and Electric Company] and described by the health department report as emitting substantial amounts of pollutants, was built in 1929 and shut in May [2006].

The shipyard, acquired by the U.S. Navy in 1940 and operated by the military until the mid-1970s, drew thousands of African American workers from the South, creating a new neighborhood on the city's southeast side, Bayview-Hunters Point. The shipyard was used for a variety of purposes, including shipbuilding and repair, submarine testing and radiological research. When it shut, many neighborhood residents were left without jobs—but with high levels of toxic substances still in the ground, water and air.

Toxins Remain

In 1989, the shipyard was listed by the federal government as a Superfund site, meaning it is extremely toxic. Parts of it, according to the public health report, "remain contaminated and unusable because of chemical pollution, radioactive waste and neglect."

The Navy is charged with cleaning up the 493-acre ship-yard before transferring it to the city, which along with a development company is beginning to overhaul the property. The Navy has spent more than $400 million on cleanup, but five of the six parcels that compose the shipyard are still on the federal Superfund list. Parcel A, the only segment deemed clean enough for development so far, will be the site of about 1,600 housing units. Other parcels won't be clean enough for development for years.

"If this area was in the Presidio, do you think it would take this long?" Pomerantz asked the students.

"No," a girl responded. "Rich people live there."

The group wound its way to the big, gray windowless building that once housed the top-secret Naval Radiological Defense Laboratory, where 600 people researched the effects of nuclear weapons. It sits next to a landfill, which was used as a dump by the Navy and has been capped without anybody fully knowing what lies within it.

His mother suffers from chronic bronchitis and he wonders whether he'll get it, too.

An investigation by the *SF Weekly* newspaper found that thousands of animals, including mice, rats, pigs and dogs, were irradiated [exposed to radiation] at the lab in science experiments and that many of their carcasses were buried in the adjacent dump. Some of their remains were placed in metal barrels and dumped near the Farallones [a group of islands off the coast of San Francisco].

"Man, it makes you think," said Eric Martin, 17. "But at the same time, it's like, what can I do to help the situation? It's very unfair."

James Ang, 17, has lived in Bayview-Hunters Point most of his life and said learning that he's been in such close proximity to toxic waste for so long scares him. His mother suffers from chronic bronchitis and he wonders whether he'll get it, too.

"We're all living in the same city, but they put it all in this neighborhood," he said. "Other neighborhoods—they could have built stuff there, but they chose not to. They are people with higher incomes, I'm guessing."

A Silver Lining

Ang said he thinks tourists should sign up to take the Toxic Tour to learn that San Francisco isn't just about its bridges, cable cars and sourdough bread.

"I think they'd take a lot in. They think San Francisco is a happy, happy place with no downsides," he said. "They don't realize how bad this area is, how polluted it is. . . . Some parts of San Francisco need help."

The Toxic Tour ends on a positive note—at Heron's Head Park, a 24-acre restored marsh near the shuttered power plant. Seventy-four species of birds live there, and student volunteers help take care of the park and learn about environmental science.

It is the future site of the Living Classroom, a 1,500-square-foot building that will be constructed in an environmentally cutting-edge fashion and serve as "the hub of education, protection and restoration for the city's southern bay shoreline," according to Literacy for Environmental Justice, which is heading the project.

The students from Downtown High sat at a picnic table as the sun began to come out, talking about what they had learned on the tour.

"It's a lot of information," Pomerantz told them. "Sometimes really heavy. Sometimes really hopeful."

12

Coal Ash Is a Threat to the Environment

Mark Guarino

Mark Guarino is a feature writer and news reporter who has worked in journalism since 1994. He writes regularly for the Chicago Daily Herald.

After a retaining wall broke at a coal-fired power plant in Tennessee in December of 2008, 5.4 million cubic yards of toxic coal ash spilled into the surrounding area, contaminating the land and water. The disaster shows that existing safety laws are insufficient and favor the energy industry. It is time to rethink waste storage and the recycling of waste, so that toxins that can cause birth defects and nervous disorders won't affect the environment and population.

Each summer, Rick Cantrell liked to pull up catfish off the dock behind his sister's house on Clinch River, a seasonal ritual that often lasts until the early hours of the morning.

That ended the Monday before Christmas [2008] when a retaining wall broke at a Tennessee Valley Authority (TVA) coal-fired power plant, releasing into the wild 5.4 million cubic yards of toxic sludge. In one day, the sludge destroyed several homes, the property values of the immediate region, and a way of life.

"There's no water anymore. There's no dock there anymore. It's all gone," said Mr. Cantrell.

Mark Guarino, "Tennessee Spill Revives Coal Ash Controversy," *Christian Science Monitor*, December 31, 2008. Reproduced by permission of the author.

Residents in this East Tennessee mountain valley of intersecting waterways and lush vistas are still adjusting to the realization that life may never be the same following what some say could be the largest environmental disaster in US history.

Laws Are in Need of Reexamination

Occurring within weeks of a new administration taking office in Washington, the disaster has brought attention to the regulation of the storage and disposal of waste coal. Environmentalists hope it will lead to a reexamination of coal as clean energy.

Photographs show hundreds of acres of land caked in what looks like thick, porous mud but is actually water-soaked coal ash, the byproduct of coal combustion. The TVA claimed about 400 acres were covered in the sludge. According to the EPA [Environmental Protection Agency], enough coal ash was released to cover more than 3,000 acres with sludge one foot deep.

"[The waste] turned one of the most beautiful places in this country into a giant slag heap," Mr. Irwin said.

The Kingston Fossil Plant at Harriman, located 40 miles west of Knoxville, is now surrounded by emergency crews, clean-up contractors, environmental groups, and homeowners, working to determine what caused the break and what harmful chemicals may have infected the water and, potentially, the air.

So far, "very high" traces of arsenic, lead, and thallium have been found in the Emory River a mile and a half downstream from the plant, said Laura Niles, spokesperson for the Environmental Protection Agency (EPA). The toxins, which are known to cause birth defects and nervous and reproductive disorders, pose significant risk since the Emory River feeds into the Clinch River and the Tennessee River.

Residents are being cautioned against drinking tap or well water, although Ms. Niles said the toxins had not yet been found near the water treatment plant near Kingston. John Moulton, spokesperson for the TVA, said the company is building an underwater rock wall at the base of the Emory River to catch sediment.

The bulk of the coal ash "is inert [not active]," he said, adding that if higher than normal levels of metal were found in the water, it would be filtered out by the treatment plant.

As sampling continues, the disaster has renewed the debate over the efficiency of coal power and the EPA's role in regulating storage and distribution of its waste.

Critics say the EPA failed to create national standards for waste storage due to opposition from utility companies and the coal industry.

Revisiting Energy Generation

At least half of all electrical power in the US is generated by coal-fired power plants, located mostly in the Southeast. In 2007, electric utilities and independent power producers consumed about 1 billion tons of coal, representing 93 percent of all coal produced in the US that year.

The high consumption results in about 125 million tons of waste, which is traditionally cooled and stored in landfills.

Critics say the EPA failed to create national standards for waste storage due to opposition from utility companies and the coal industry. With responsibility handed off to state agencies, standards vary widely, resulting in the phenomenon of "importing pollution" from a highly regulated state to one with lower standards, according to Carrie La Seur, president of Plains Justice, an environmental law center in Cedar Rapids, Iowa.

"It's really been a federal failure to regulate this waste stream that has resulted in this patchwork," said Ms. La Seur.

"You get . . . a 'race to the bottom.' Every state has the perverse incentive to create the loosest regulation to attract whatever businesses are available."

Because the EPA was reluctant to classify coal ash as hazardous during the [President Bill] Clinton administration, companies are not required to store coal ash in lined landfills. The Kingston facility stores its waste in unlined ponds with just a retaining wall separating it from the Emory River.

TVA's Mr. Moulton said the company is reconsidering how coal ash is stored and disposed at the Kingston plant.

Due to the sheer volume of waste produced, the coal industry has been advocating recycling the material into backfill and building materials such as cement, bricks, or wallboard.

About 60 percent of the approximately 600 coal plants in the US are designed to recycle coal waste, unlike older plants like Kingston, says David Goss, executive director of the American Coal Ash Association. But only about 45 percent of coal ash gets reused.

"It's not the norm yet," said Mr. Goss, adding that that is likely to change as utility companies realize the revenue potential of marketing their waste for byproducts. However, it's not clear if coal ash can be effectively recycled without leaching toxins into groundwater or the air.

13

Coal Ash Is More Radioactive than Nuclear Waste

Mara Hvistendahl

Mara Hvistendahl is a Shanghai-based writer. Her work has appeared in Harper's, *the* Financial Times *magazine, the* New Republic, *and other publications.*

Contrary to popular belief, the waste from coal plants is more radioactive than that from nuclear plants. And fly ash is carried into the environment, endangering the public. This adds to the ongoing rivalry between the different forms of energy production. Although coal plants don't pose the risk of catastrophic malfunctions, the day-to-day pollution and radiation emitted might be higher.

The popular conception of nuclear power is straight out of *The Simpsons*: Springfield abounds with signs of radioactivity, from the strange glow surrounding Mr. Burn's nuclear power plant workers to Homer's low sperm count. Then there's the local superhero, Radioactive Man, who fires beams of "nuclear heat" from his eyes. Nuclear power, many people think, is inseparable from a volatile, invariably lime-green, mutant-making radioactivity.

Coal, meanwhile, is believed responsible for a host of more quotidian problems, such as mining accidents, acid rain and greenhouse gas emissions. But it isn't supposed to spawn three-eyed fish like Blinky.

Mara Hvistendahl, "Coal Ash Is More Radioactive than Nuclear Waste," *Scientific American,* December 13, 2007. Copyright © 2007 by Scientific American, Inc. All rights reserved. Reproduced by permission of the author.

Over the past few decades, however, a series of studies has called these stereotypes into question. Among the surprising conclusions: the waste produced by coal plants is actually more radioactive than that generated by their nuclear counterparts. In fact, the fly ash emitted by a power plant—a byproduct from burning coal for electricity—carries into the surrounding environment 100 times more radiation than a nuclear power plant producing the same amount of energy.* [*See Editor's Note at end of page 2*]

At issue is coal's content of uranium and thorium, both radioactive elements. They occur in such trace amounts in natural, or "whole," coal that they aren't a problem. But when coal is burned into fly ash; uranium and thorium are concentrated at up to 10 times their original levels.

Fly ash uranium sometimes leaches into the soil and water surrounding a coal plant, affecting cropland and, in turn, food. People living within a "stack shadow"—the area within a half- to one-mile (0.8- to 1.6-kilometer) radius of a coal plant's smokestacks—might then ingest small amounts of radiation. Fly ash is also disposed of in landfills and abandoned mines and quarries, posing a potential risk to people living around those areas.

When coal is burned into fly ash, uranium and thorium are concentrated at up to 10 times their original levels.

In a 1978 paper for *Science*, J. P. McBride at Oak Ridge National Laboratory (ORNL) and his colleagues looked at the uranium and thorium content of fly ash from coal-fired power plants in Tennessee and Alabama. To answer the question of just how harmful leaching could be, the scientists estimated radiation exposure around the coal plants and compared it with exposure levels around boiling-water reactor and pressurized-water nuclear power plants.

The result: estimated radiation doses ingested by people living near the coal plants were equal to or higher than doses for people living around the nuclear facilities. At one extreme, the scientists estimated fly ash radiation in individuals' bones at around 18 millirems (thousandths of a rem, a unit for measuring doses of ionizing radiation) a year. Doses for the two nuclear plants, by contrast, ranged from between three and six millirems for the same period. And when all food was grown in the area, radiation doses were 50 to 200 percent higher around the coal plants.

McBride and his co-authors estimated that individuals living near coal-fired installations are exposed to a maximum of 1.9 millirems of fly ash radiation yearly. To put these numbers in perspective, the average person encounters 360 millirems of annual "background radiation" from natural and man-made sources, including substances in Earth's crust, cosmic rays, residue from nuclear tests and smoke detectors.

Dana Christensen, associate lab director for energy and engineering at ORNL, says that health risks from radiation in coal by-products are low. "Other risks like being hit by lightning," he adds, "are three or four times greater than radiation-induced health effects from coal plants." And McBride and his co-authors emphasize that other products of coal power, like emissions of acid rain-producing sulfur dioxide and smog-forming nitrous oxide, pose greater health risks than radiation.

The U.S. Geological Survey (USGS) maintains an online database of fly ash-based uranium content for sites across the U.S. In most areas, the ash contains less uranium than some common rocks. In Tennessee's Chattanooga shale, for example, there is more uranium in phosphate rock.

Robert Finkelman, a former USGS coordinator of coal quality who oversaw research on uranium in fly ash in the 1990s, says that for the average person the by-product accounts for a minuscule amount of background radiation, probably less than 0.1 percent of total background radiation exposure. According to USGS calculations, buying a house in a stack shadow—in this case within 0.6 mile [one kilometer] of a coal plant—increases the annual amount of radiation you're exposed to by a maximum of 5 percent. But that's still less than the radiation encountered in normal yearly exposure to X-rays.

"The miners are surrounded by rocks and sloshing through ground water that is exuding radon."

So why does coal waste appear so radioactive? It's a matter of comparison: The chances of experiencing adverse health effects from radiation are slim for both nuclear and coal-fired power plants—they're just somewhat higher for the coal ones. "You're talking about one chance in a billion for nuclear power plants," Christensen says. "And it's one in 10 million to one in a hundred million for coal plants."

Radiation from uranium and other elements in coal might only form a genuine health risk to miners, Finkelman explains. "It's more of an occupational hazard than a general environmental hazard," he says. "The miners are surrounded by rocks and sloshing through ground water that is exuding radon."

Developing countries like India and China continue to unveil new coal-fired plants—at the rate of one every seven to 10 days in the latter nation. And the U.S. still draws around half of its electricity from coal. But coal plants have an additional strike against them: they emit harmful greenhouse gases.

With the world now focused on addressing climate change, nuclear power is gaining favor in some circles. China aims to quadruple nuclear capacity to 40,000 megawatts by 2020, and the U.S. may build as many as 30 new reactors in the next several decades. But, although the risk of a nuclear core meltdown is very low, the impact of such an event creates a stigma around the noncarbon power source.

The question boils down to the accumulating impacts of daily incremental pollution from burning coal or the small risk but catastrophic consequences of even one nuclear melt-down. "I suspect we'll hear more about this rivalry," Finkelman says. "More coal will be mined in the future. And those ignorant of the issues, or those who have a vested interest in other forms of energy, may be tempted to raise these issues again."

Editor's Note (posted 12/30/08): In response to some concerns raised by readers, a change has been made to this story. The sentence marked with an asterisk was changed from "In fact, fly ash—a by-product from burning coal for power—and other coal waste contains up to 100 times more radiation than nuclear waste" to "In fact, the fly ash emitted by a power plant—a by-product from burning coal for electricity—carries into the surrounding environment 100 times more radiation than a nuclear power plant producing the same amount of energy." Our source for this statistic is Dana Christensen, an associate lab director for energy and engineering at Oak Ridge National Laboratory as well as 1978 paper in Science *authored by J.P. McBride and colleagues, also of ORNL.*

As a general clarification, ounce for ounce, coal ash released from a power plant delivers more radiation than nuclear waste shielded via water or dry cask storage.

14

Toxic Waste Finds Its Way into Food

Boyd Harnell

Boyd Harnell formerly worked with Time Life TV, UPI, ABC *print media division, and as an editor with* Kyodo News Japan. *Currently, Harnell works as an investigative reporter with the* Japan Times. *His articles on Japan's secret dolphin slaughter led to two International Genesis Awards, jointly, with JT Features Editor Andrew Kershaw.*

The practice of slaughtering thousands of Dolphins annually has often been condemned by Western media, but Japan has continued the custom and provided dolphin meat for school lunches. Yet the mercury levels found in the dolphin meat are unsafe, and could harm children. Although researchers warn against the consumption of dolphin meat, politicians and public officials will not broach the subject out of fear of upsetting the fishing industry. Yet dolphin meat has probably already harmed consumers, and can no longer be eaten safely.

For what is believed to be the first time anywhere in Japan, elected officials have openly condemned the consumption of dolphin meat, especially in school lunches, on grounds that it is dangerously contaminated with mercury.

In an exclusive interview with *The Japan Times* held in Kii Katsuura, Wakayama Prefecture, on July 19 [2007], Assembly-

Boyd Harnell, "Taiji Officials: Dolphin Meat 'Toxic Waste,'" *The Japan Times*, August 1, 2007; "'Toxic Waste': Why Bother to Set Mercury Limits That Are Ignored?" *The Japan Times*, March 30, 2008. Copyright © 2007, 2008 *The Japan Times*. All rights reserved. Both reproduced by permission of the author.

men Junichiro Yamashita, 59, and Hisato Ryono, 51, from the nearby whaling city of Taiji said they had found extremely high mercury and methylmercury levels in samples of meat from pilot whales killed inshore by Taiji hunters and put on sale in that locality.

The pilot whale, or "gondou" (Globicephala macro-rhynchus), is next to the largest of the dolphin family of small cetaceans [mammals adapted to aquatic life]—Orca being the largest. The gondou dolphin species is among some 2,300 dolphins slaughtered annually in Taiji, after the mammals are herded in "drive fisheries" into small coves, where they are speared and hacked to death. Similar hunts elsewhere in Japan are estimated to account for at least another 20,000 small cetaceans annually.

The Taiji assemblymen, who are both independents, also condemned the growing practice of feeding this meat to children in their school lunches—describing it as no less than "toxic waste."

The random samples tested by the two assemblymen were bought at supermarkets in Taiji and nearby Shingu, and were similarly sourced to the meat served to children in whale-meat lunches at Taiji schools. Such lunches may also have been served in schools in other prefectures, the Taiji officials said.

Yamashita and Ryono defied the code of silence traditionally shrouding sensitive issues, especially one that could threaten the economy of their small, isolated fishing town on the scenic Kii Peninsula.

Asked why, they said local people were getting very anxious about food safety in Japan. Recent reports of contaminated products from China have heightened their concerns, they said.

Yamashita explained, "We're not against traditional whaling, but we heard claims that pilot whales are poisoned with mercury, and we discovered that some of this meat from a (drive fishery) was fed to kids in school lunches."

He said that although they had doubted the pilot whales were contaminated with mercury, they decided to have certified lab tests carried out nonetheless.

"We tested some samples—purchased at the Gyokyo supermarket in Taiji and Super Center Okuwa in the nearby city of Shingu," Yamashita said, adding they were "shocked" by the results.

One dolphin sample had a mercury content 10 times above the health ministry's advisory level of 0.4 parts per million, with a methylmercury readout 10.33 times over the ministry's own advisory level of 0.3 ppm.

Another dolphin sample tested 15.97 times and 12 times above advisory levels of total mercury and methylmercury, respectively.

The results prompted the two officials to describe dolphin meat as "toxic waste."

In fact, the dolphin levels were higher than some of the mercury-tainted seafood tested during the tragic Minamata mercury-pollution disaster of the 1950s, according to Dr. Shigeo Ekino of Kumamoto Medical Science University in Kyushu. In that episode, thousands were sickened, disabled or died in the toxic chemical disaster.

Ekino is famous for his breakthrough study of brain specimens from deceased Minamata disease victims that reveals how even low levels of methylmercury can damage or destroy neurons.

The results prompted the two officials to describe dolphin meat as "toxic waste."

After they received the test results, the Taiji lawmakers, anxious about the possible toxic effects of pilot-whale meat consumed by local schoolchildren, quickly contacted Masahiko Tamaki, an official of the Wakayama prefectural health section, and showed him the test results from their samples.

Yamashita said, "He (Tamaki) seems to think he has to do something, but doesn't know how to do it."

Tamaki was hesitant to confront the mercury issue due to possible repercussions, and offered no solutions, Yamashita said, adding, "The Wakayama health section simply told me they didn't want to upset Taiji people."

But Yamashita said: "According to the high mercury result, if they continue, the people will be harmed—this harm, spread through school lunches, is terrible because children will be forced to eat mercury-tainted dolphin."

Despite the Taiji pair's urgent health concerns, however, Taiji Mayor Kazutaka Sangen plans to build a new slaughterhouse for processing meat from pilot whales and other dolphins caught during globally condemned drive fisheries there.

He also wants to expand the provision of school lunches containing pilot whale meat.

Top researchers in Japan's medical community have . . . voiced concern about the high levels of mercury found in small-cetacean food products.

Ryono said, "We may not be able to prevent the building of a new slaughterhouse, but we will continue to appeal to Taiji people not to use dolphin for school lunches."

Meanwhile, concern over 12 dolphins currently in "capture pens" in Taiji is mounting as the mammals await imminent shipment to a dolphin aquarium in the Dominican Republic. This has prompted Yamashita and Ryono to write an urgent letter to Max Puig, environmental minister of the Dominican Republic, protesting importation of the dolphins, saying his environmentally friendly island state would be accepting "toxic waste." Ultimately, the island state refused to accept the dolphins based on mercury findings by the Taiji officials and massive petitions protesting the imports organized by the Save Japan Dolphins coalition.

Top researchers in Japan's medical community have also voiced concern about the high levels of mercury found in small-cetacean food products.

Ekino told *The Japan Times*: "Everyone should avoid eating dolphin meat. If people continue to eat dolphin, there's a high probability of them having damage to their brains.... No government agency is studying the problem—no scientists in Japan want to study the subject; it's very political."

Award-winning U.S. neurologist David Perlmutter echoed Ekino's sentiments in a telephone interview, saying, "I totally agree with Dr. Ekino when he said everyone should avoid eating dolphin meat—the consumption of dolphin meat is a profound health risk for humans."

Referring to Japan's health advisories warning pregnant women that consuming dolphin meat "can be harmful to the fetus and to young children," Perlmutter, who has a private practice at his clinic in Naples, Fla., said, "If it's a risk for pregnant women and children, why is it safe for anyone else?"

Tetsuya Endo, a professor and researcher at Hokkaido Health Science University's faculty of pharmaceutical sciences, affirmed the other doctors' condemnation of small-cetacean food products.

In a terse e-mail sent to this correspondent, Endo said, in reference to dolphin meat, "It's not food!"

In 2005, Endo published the results of a three-year study on random samples of cetacean food products sold throughout Japan, and concluded all of it was unhealthy because of high levels of mercury and methylmercury.

However, Hideki Moronuki, deputy director of the government's Far Seas Fisheries Division of the Resources Management Department, in an interview with *The Japan*

Times, maligned Endo's study, calling it "misleading information." When pressed, though, he failed to substantiate his accusation.

Endo, however, responded to *The Japan Times* in an e-mail, saying, "If he (Moronuki) has any basis for his comments, he has the responsibility to show it because it is deeply related to human health."

Moronuki was specifically asked if there was a mercury problem with dolphins. His response: "No."

He acknowledged that doctors' reports (of high mercury levels) may be correct, but claimed, "I don't think it causes a problem with consumers."

When asked if he thought consuming dolphin meat was dangerous, he said, "No."

But he conceded that eating too much dolphin meat could be "dangerous."

Moronuki was also asked if he felt responsible for the poisoning of his own people. He replied: "No. I am responsible for the management of the dolphin fishery, that's it."

This bureaucrat's attitude flies in the face of certified copies of six test reports commissioned and paid for over the past year, each showing high mercury levels in the meat put on sale from all dolphin species tested. That data [has] been made freely available by *The Japan Times* to the appropriate Japanese government agencies and officials.

Despite this hard data, government authorities have consistently displayed a sense of apathy toward these matters, and what many informed commentators regard as dangerously cavalier attitudes in dealing with urgent health issues affecting their citizens.

Makoto Tanaka, assistant director of the health ministry's inspection and safety division in the Food Safety Department, would only say that he is seeking an international standard for establishing a new advisory level for consumers of mercury-tainted food products.

The health ministry has been aware of the mercury problem in small cetaceans (not to mention in the meat from great whales) for many years, but so far it has refused to ban the sale of such food products.

In particular—despite unequivocal scientific test results—it has failed to require the posting of warning labels for consumers of dolphin meat.

This approach continues despite an advisory order, Kan Nyu Dai 99 Ban, established July 23, 1973, under which a warning was issued to prefectural and local governments by the then director of the environmental and health agency, stating that mercury in seafood must not exceed the advisory level of 0.4 ppm.

Although still in effect, enforcement of the advisory order by governors and mayors has been lax and unchallenged.

But the reaction around the killing coves of Taiji was swift in confronting the two assemblymen's health concerns.

On the one hand, Gyokyo, the leading local supermarket, pulled pilot whale meat off its shelves, and will not resume its sale, according to Takuya Kondo, assistant director of the health ministry's Department of Food Safety's Standards and Evaluation Division.

Kondo said, "The (Taiji) government has to comply with . . . provisional regulations. . . . They are not supposed to sell (dolphin meat) if it is over the advisory level of 0.4 ppm for mercury."

Yamashita and Ryono believe many people in Japan are unaware of the (health) problems related to consuming dolphin meat, and they say they want to educate people through an Internet blog currently posted by the Save Japan Dolphins coalition, an international conservation group.

But it would be a lot more straightforward if this issue was addressed in a more open and accountable way by officials.

Instead, a pervasive sense of paranoia seems to loom over any investigation of the mercury contamination of foodstuff in Japan.

On this reporter's initial visit to the test lab, my sample of dolphin meat was at first rejected for testing by lab officials, who greeted me with a file of my articles on the barbaric dolphin slaughter in Taiji, and the toxicity of cetacean meat sold in Japan.

One lab official said: "Sometimes happens big problem, I must confirm your purpose. . . . We cannot stand in opposite position of Fishery Agency. . . . If you publish our report, we'll have to close the lab."

A pervasive sense of paranoia seems to loom over any investigation of the mercury contamination of foodstuff in Japan.

The lab later conducted the test after learning the test-sample result would determine whether a potentially dangerous public-health hazard existed.

Also, during the dolphin drives and the animals' subsequent slaughter in Taiji, I was followed nonstop by the Taiji Isana group's self appointed security guard and prime stalker. Kazutoyo Simetani, who was in my shadow wherever I went. Shingu police also attempted to question me several times, especially Kazuhiro Sasaki, and, to my considerable consternation, he seemed to know my name exactly as written on my driver's license—even though only my hotel had a copy of my license. Without probable cause of a crime being committed, this constitutes a major breach of my privacy, which is supposed to be strictly enforced in Japan—but this infraction and blatant violations of Japan's free press law—seem to be subjectively decided by local law enforcement.

It was very unsettling.

Perhaps the two courageous assemblymen may have sounded the final death knell to Japan's dolphin slaughter by focusing the spotlight on the toxic products of this butchery.

But how many Japanese may already be adversely affected, so many years after the danger of this cruel trade has been known?

Update: Hisato Ryono has since reversed his position and again sits on the Taiji City Council. He currently supports the drive fisheries.

Addendum: "Toxic Waste": Why Bother to Set Mercury Limits That Are Ignored?

The following are the results of certified and documented tests of Total Mercury (T-Hg) found in random samples of dolphin meat purchased from supermarkets in Taiji and Shingu, Wakayama Prefecture, in 2006–2008.

The test system used is known as Cold Vapor Atomic Absorption Spectrometry.

The following are the results of certified and documented tests of Total Mercury and Methylmercury in samples of dolphin meat bought at local supermarkets in Taiji and Shingu, Wakayama, Japan. After receiving results of the tests, Taiji city assemblyman Junichiro Yamashita described the dolphin meat as "toxic waste" and urged his constituents not to consume it on grounds of health.

The Health, Labor and Welfare Ministry's safe advisory level for T-Hg is 0.4 ppm (parts per million) and the health ministry's safe advisory level for Methylmercury (M-Hg) is 0.3 ppm (parts per million).

1. Tested sample (11/07/06): Gondou dolphin (pilot whale); T-Hg 1.31 ppm (3.3 times the Japanese government's advisory level)

2. Tested sample (11/07/06): Gondou dolphin (pilot whale); T-Hg 3.82 ppm (9.55 times the advisory level)

3. Tested sample (12/22/06): Striped dolphin; T-Hg 5.40 ppm (13.5 times the advisory level)

4. Tested sample (2/23/06): Bottlenose dolphin; T-Hg 1.7 ppm (4 times the advisory level)

5. Tested sample (3/02/07): Common dolphin; T-Hg 1.66 ppm (4 times the advisory level)

6. Tested sample (3/02/07): Striped dolphin; T-Hg 14.3 ppm (35.75 times the advisory level)

7. Tested sample (6/22/07): Gondou dolphin (pilot whale); T-Hg 6.39 ppm (15.97 times the advisory level); M-Hg 3.6 ppm (12 times the advisory level)

8. Tested sample (7/17/07): Gondou dolphin (pilot whale); T-Hg 11.9 ppm (29.75 times the advisory level); M-Hg 4.8 ppm (16 times the advisory level)

9. Tested sample (8/02/07): Gondou dolphin (pilot whale); T-Hg 3.84 ppm (9.6 times the advisory level)

10. Tested sample (10/2/07): Gondou dolphin (pilot whale); T-Hg 10.4 ppm (26 times the advisory level)

11. Tested sample (10/12/07): Gondou dolphin (pilot whale); T-Hg 6.94 ppm (7.35 times the advisory level)

Organizations to Contact

The editors have compiled the following list of organizations concerned with the issues debated in this book. The descriptions are derived from materials provided by the organizations. All have publications or information available for interested readers. The list was compiled on the date of publication of the present volume; the information provided here may change. Be aware that many organizations take several weeks or longer to respond to inquiries, so allow as much time as possible.

Collective Heritage Institute (CHI)
1607 Paseo De Peralta #3, Santa Fe, NM 87501
(877) 246-6337 • Fax: (505) 986-1644
E-mail: info@bioneers.org
Web site: www.bioneers.org

The Collective Heritage Institute conducts education and research in the areas of biodiversity, ecological farming practices, and environmental restoration. Founded in 1990, CHI projects include the annual Bioneers Conference and the Restorative Development Initiative. News stories and radio shows are available online.

Greenpeace
702 H Street NW, Suite 300, Washington, DC 20001
(202) 462-1177
Web site: www.greenpeace.org

Greenpeace is working to combat some of the most dangerous threats to the environment, such as global warming, overfishing, toxic pollution, and the destruction of ancient forests, in a peaceful, nonviolent manner. Greenpeace makes news stories and educational texts available on its Web site, and also informs the public via Twitter.

Interfaith Center on Corporate Responsibility (ICCR)
475 Riverside Drive, Suite 1842, New York, NY 10115
(212) 870-2295 • Fax: (212) 870-2023
E-mail: info@iccr.org
Web site: www.iccr.org

ICCR's Energy & Environment Program focuses on helping religious investors challenge companies on environmental policies and the economic impacts of irresponsible corporate citizenship. Through the power of investors' shares, companies are pressed to listen to religious stakeholders' concerns in developing responsible corporate behavior. ICCR offers newsletters, published articles, briefs, presentations, and books via its Web site.

Interfaith Partnership for the Environment—A Project of the United Nations Environment Programme (Regional Office for North America) (UNEP/RONA)
900 17th Street NW, Washington, DC 20006
(202) 785-0465 • Fax: (202) 785-2096
Web site: www.rona.unep.org

The Interfaith Partnership for the Environment was organized for the purpose of involving the world's religions in the growing struggle to preserve the Earth's environment for future generations. An environmental Sabbath was held in June 1987, and the book *Only One Earth* was created for the event. Over 10 years, 60,000 copies of the book have been given free to religious organizations, universities, and schools throughout the world. An updated version is now available.

International Atomic Energy Agency (IAEA)
1 United Nations Plaza, Room DC-1-1155
New York, NY 10017
(212) 963-6010 or 6011 • Fax: (917) 367-4046
E-mail: iaeany@un.org
Web site: www.iaea.org

The IAEA is the world's center of cooperation in the nuclear field. It was set up as the world's "Atoms for Peace" organization in 1957 within the United Nations family. The agency works with its member states and multiple partners world-wide to promote safe, secure, and peaceful nuclear technologies. The IAEA is a leading publisher in the nuclear field. Its scientific and technical publications cover fifteen subject areas. They include proceedings of major international conferences, as well as international guides, codes, and standards.

National Association of Energy Service Companies (NAESCO)

1615 M Street NW, Suite 800, Washington, DC   20036
(202) 822-0950 • Fax: (202) 822-0955
Web site: www.naesco.org

Members include individuals and firms providing energy efficiency services or electrical or thermal energy as an unregulated business activity by using a range of performance-based contracting and financing mechanisms, and nonprofit and government bodies interested in the energy service industry. The purpose is to provide industry representation at all regulatory and government levels. NAESCO serves as an information clearinghouse through its bimonthly publication, *Energy Efficiency Journal.*

National Energy Education Development Project (NEED)

8408 Kao Circle, Manassas, VA   20110
(703) 257-1117 • Fax: (703) 257-0037
E-mail: info@need.org
Web site: www.need.org

NEED is a national network of students, educators, and leaders in government and industry dedicated to providing comprehensive energy programming. Through hands-on science, math, drama, social science, art, and music, students work with their peers, teachers, family, and community on energy education programs they design themselves. NEED publishes curriculum resources for students and teachers.

National Mining Association (NMA)

101 Constitution Ave. NW, Suite 500 East
Washington, DC   20001-2133
(202) 463-2600 • Fax: (202) 463-2666
E-mail: craulston@nma.org
Web site: www.nma.org

The National Mining Association serves as the information center for the United States mining industry, as well as the political presence for mining in Washington. The association works closely with Congress, the executive branch, and federal agencies to ensure the establishment of constructive policies that will best enable the mining industry to serve the needs of the nation. NMA publishes many newsletters and reports that can be downloaded from its Web site.

National Petrochemical & Refiners Association (NPRA)

1667 K Street NW, Suite 700, Washington, DC   20006
(202) 457-0480 • Fax: (202) 457-0486
E-mail: info@npradc.org
Web site: www.npradc.org

The National Petrochemical & Refiners Association represents almost 500 companies, virtually all U.S. refiners and petrochemical manufacturers. Members work to operate their facilities safely and to protect human health and the environment. Newsletters are available online.

Nuclear Energy Institute (NEI)

1776 I Street NW, Suite 400, Washington, DC   20006-3708
(202) 739-8000 • Fax: (202) 785-4019
Web site: www.nei.org

NEI's objective is to ensure the formation of policies that promote the beneficial uses of nuclear energy and technologies in the United States and around the world. Its membership includes companies that operate nuclear power plants, design and engineering firms, fuel suppliers and service companies, companies involved in nuclear medicine and nuclear industrial applications, radionuclide and radiopharmaceutical companies, universities and research laboratories, and labor unions. Studies and a document library are offered online.

Sierra Club
85 Second Street, Second Floor, San Francisco, CA   94105
(415) 977-5500 • Fax: (415) 977-5799
E-mail: information@sierraclub.org
Web site: www.sierraclub.org

The Sierra Club is a nonprofit, member-supported, public-interest organization that promotes conservation of the natural environment by influencing public policy decisions—legislative, administrative, legal, and electoral. News stories and educational materials are available on its Web site.

Worldwatch Institute
1776 Massachusetts Ave. NW, Washington, DC   20036
(202) 452-1999 • Fax: (202) 296-7365
E-mail: worldwatch@worldwatch.org
Web site: www.worldwatch.org

Worldwatch is a nonprofit public policy research organization dedicated to informing policy makers and the public about emerging global problems and trends and the complex links between the world economy and its environmental support systems. Articles and books are available on its Web site.

Bibliography

Books

Richard Andrews — *Managing the Environment, Managing Ourselves: A History of American Environmental Policy.* 2nd ed. New Haven, CT: Yale University Press, 2006.

Nicholas Ashford and Charles Caldart — *Environmental Law, Policy and Economics: Reclaiming the Environmental Agenda.* Cambridge, MA: MIT Press, 2008.

Edmund Burke III and Kenneth Pomeranz, eds. — *The Environment and World History.* Berkeley, CA: University of California Press, 2009.

Neil Carter — *The Politics of the Environment: Ideas, Activism, Policy.* 2nd ed. New York, NY: Cambridge University Press, 2007.

Steven Cohen — *Understanding Environmental Policy.* Irvington, NY: Columbia University Press, 2006.

Susan Cragin — *Nuclear Nebraska: The Remarkable Story of the Little County That Couldn't Be Bought.* New York, NY: AMACOM, 2007.

Thomas Dunlap — *Faith in Nature: Environmentalism as Religious Quest.* Seattle, WA: University of Washington Press, 2005.

Robert F. Durant, Daniel Fiorino, and Rosemary O'Leary — *Environmental Governance Reconsidered: Challenges, Choices, and Opportunities.* Cambridge, MA: MIT Press, 2004.

Marc Allen Eisner — *Governing the Environment: The Transformation of Environmental Regulation.* Boulder, CO: Lynne Rienner, 2006.

Daniel Fiorino — *The New Environmental Regulation.* Cambridge, MA: MIT Press, 2006.

Michael Greenberg, et al. — *The Reporter's Handbook on Nuclear Materials, Energy, and Waste Management.* Nashville, TN: Vanderbilt University Press, 2009.

Joy Hecht — *National Environmental Accounting: Bridging the Gap Between Ecology and Economy.* Washington, DC: Resources for the Future, 2004.

Bruce E. Johansen — *The Dirty Dozen: Toxic Chemicals and the Earth's Future.* Santa Barbara, CA: Praeger, 2008.

Genevieve Johnson — *Deliberative Democracy for the Future: The Case of Nuclear Waste Management in Canada.* Toronto, ON: University of Toronto Press, 2008.

Pradyumna Karan and Unryu Suganuma, eds. — *Local Environmental Movements: A Comparative Study of the United States and Japan.* Lexington, KY: University Press of Kentucky, 2008.

Andrew Kirk	*Counterculture Green: The Whole Earth Catalog and American Environmentalism.* Lawrence, KS: University Press of Kansas, 2007.
Michael Kraft and Sheldon Kamieniecki, eds.	*Business and Environmental Policy: Corporate Interests in the American Political System.* Cambridge, MA: MIT Press, 2007.
Charles Krebs	*The Ecological World View.* Berkeley, CA: University of California Press, 2008.
Gerald Markowitz and David Rosner	*Deceit and Denial: The Deadly Politics of Industrial Pollution.* Berkeley, CA: University of California Press, 2002.
Brian Mayer	*Blue-Green Coalitions: Fighting for Safe Workplaces and Healthy Communities.* Ithaca, NY: Cornell University Press, 2008.
Donella Meadows, Jorgen Randers, and Dennis Meadows	*The Limits to Growth.* White River Junction, VT: Chelsea Green, 2004.
Chad Montrie	*Making a Living: Work and Environment in the United States.* Chapel Hill, NC: University of North Carolina Press, 2008.
M.I. Ojovan and W.E. Lee	*An Introduction to Nuclear Waste Immobilisation.* Maryland Heights, MO: Elsevier Science, 2005.

David Pellow

Resisting Global Toxics: Transnational Movements for Environmental Justice. Cambridge, MA: MIT Press, 2007.

Harold Platt

Shock Cities: The Environmental Transformation and Reform of Manchester and Chicago. Chicago, IL: University of Chicago Press, 2005.

Sarah Pralle

Branching Out, Digging In: Environmental Advocacy and Agenda Setting. Washington, DC: Georgetown University Press, 2006.

Robert Repetto, ed.

Punctuated Equilibrium and the Dynamics of U.S. Environmental Policy. New Haven, CT: Yale University Press, 2006.

Peter Riley

Nuclear Waste: Law, Policy, and Pragmatism. Farnham, UK: Ashgate, 2004.

Piero Risoluti

Nuclear Waste: A Technological and Political Challenge. New York, NY: Springer, 2004.

Walter Rosenbaum

Environmental Politics and Policy. 7th ed. Washington, DC: CQ Press, 2007.

James Gustave Speth

The Bridge at the Edge of the World: Capitalism, the Environment, and Crossing from Crisis to Sustainability. New Haven, CT: Yale University Press, 2008.

Andrew Szasz   *Shopping Our Way to Safety: How We Changed from Protecting the Environment to Protecting Ourselves.* Minneapolis, MN: University of Minnesota Press, 2007.

Kerry Whiteside   *Precautionary Politics: Principle and Politics in Confronting Environmental Risk.* Cambridge, MA: MIT Press, 2006.

Periodicals

Birmingham Post   "Waste Still an Issue as Stockpile Builds Ever Upwards," *Birmingham Post* (England), January 11, 2008.

Robert Bullard, et. al.   "Toxic Waste and Race at Twenty: 1987–2007," *United Church of Christ Justice and Peace Ministry*, March 2007.

Matthew Bunn and Anthony Wier   "The Seven Myths of Nuclear Terrorism," *Current History*, April 2005.

Karen Charman   "Brave Nuclear World? The Planet Is Warming, and Proponents of Nuclear Power Say They've Got the Answer. Are Nuclear Plants the Climate Cavalry?" *World Watch*, May–June 2006.

Maria Cone   "Dozens of Chemicals Found in Most Americans' Bodies," *Los Angeles Times*, July 22, 2005.

Kay Drey   "Earth City Threatened by Migration
                    of Radioactive Waste," *St. Louis
                    Journalism Review*, February 2007.

Tasha Eichenseher   "Haste Makes Waste: Are We Paying
                    for Cut-Rate, Shoddy Military
                    Cleanup?" *E/The Environmental
                    Magazine*, November 2003.

Dinyar Godrej   "Toxic Souvenirs: Depleted Uranium
                    Weapons Have Left Behind a Trail of
                    Human Misery and Vituperative
                    Debate. What's Not Known About
                    Them Is Just as Disturbing as What
                    Is, Discovers Dinyar Godrej," *New
                    Internationalist*, November 2007.

Ed Hiserodt   "Nuclear Waste: Not a Problem:
                    Unbeknownst to Most People, the
                    Bulk of Nuclear Waste Is Recyclable,
                    and the Remainder Can Be Safely
                    Stored and Presents Little Danger to
                    Anyone," *New American*, February 18,
                    2008.

Ed Hiserodt   "Myths About Nuclear Energy," *New
                    American*, April 30, 2007.

John Johnston   "Waste Management Finds Solution
                    to Settler's Hill Toxins," *Daily Herald*
                    (Arlington Heights, IL), September
                    15, 2006.

The Journal   "Toxic Waste Requires Safe, Legal
                    Disposal; Waste and Recycling," *The
                    Journal* (Newcastle, England), August
                    20, 2007.

Jonathan Leake and Dan Box	"The Nuclear Charm Offensive: We Are All Being Taken in by a Carefully Planned Public Relations Strategy. Its Mission: To Push Nuclear Power Back on the Political Agenda, Rebranded as the New 'Green' Alternative," *New Statesman*, May 23, 2005.
Paul Lorenzini	"A Second Look at Nuclear Power: By Overlooking Nuclear Power in the Quest for Clean Energy, We Are Condemning Ourselves to a Future of Increased Fossil Fuel Use," *Issues in Science and Technology*, March 22, 2005.
Mark Lynas	"Nuclear Power: A Convert; Mark Lynas Was Sure It Would Be a Disaster—And Then He Looked at the Alternatives," *New Statesman*, May 30, 2005.
The Mirror	"Chuck This Toxic Waste," *The Mirror* (London, England), September 8, 2007.
Veronique Mistiaen	"Saving the Sacred Sea: Russian Nuclear Plant Threatens Ancient Lake," *New Internationalist*, May 2008.
Tim Montague	"A New Way to Inherit Environmental Harm," *Rachel's Environment and Health News*, June 9, 2005.

New Statesman   "The Toxic Legacy of a Nuclear
                       Future," *New Statesman*, July 17,
                       2006.

Manuel Pastor,   "In the Wake of the Storm:
et. al   Environment, Disaster and Race After
                       Katrina," *Russell Sage Foundation*,
                       May 15, 2006.

Max Schulz, Brice   "Nuclear Power: Both Sides," *Wilson
Smith, and Arjun   Quarterly*, Autumn 2006.
Makhijani

Michael Shore   "Out of Control and Close to Home:
                       Mercury Pollution from Power
                       Plants," *Environmental Defense*, 2003.

Linda Sikkema   "Nuclear Renaissance? Many Are
and Melinda   Looking at Nuclear Energy as a
Savage   Solution to Our Energy Needs and
                       Foreign Oil Dependency," *State
                       Legislatures*, March 2007.

Washington Times   "Poor Indians Recycle Harmful
                       'E-Waste' into Cash; Old Computers
                       Stripped; Industry Lacks
                       Regulations," *Washington Times*,
                       August 11, 2007.

Washington Times   "Toxic Waste Adds to Ivorian Woes,"
                       Washington Times, September 28,
                       2006.

Washington Times   "Toxic Waste in TV Transition;
                       Analog Sets Sent to Developing
                       Countries for Hazardous, Low-Paid
                       Dismantling," *Washington Times*,
                       March 16, 2008.

William Weil and the Science Advisory Committee of the Michigan Environmental Council and Ecology Center	"Guarding Michigan's Most Vulnerable: Making Michigan a Leader in Protecting Children from Environmental Pollution," *Ecology Center*, August 2002.
Vicki Wolf	"Global Chemical Contamination Threatens Child Development," *Environmental News Network*, August 19, 2005.

Index

General Electric (GE), 49

Genetically modified organisms, 65–68

Geological repositories, 16, 56–57

George Mason University, 45

Gobi Desert, 38

Goss, David, 81

Greenhouse gases, 82, 85

Greenpeace, 10–13, 67

Guarino, Mark, 78–81

H

Hannum, William H., 49

Harnell, Boyd, 87–96

Health, Labor and Welfare Ministry of Japan, 95

Hexavalent chromium, 66

Hokkaido Health Science University (Japan), 91

Hooker Chemical, 7

Hospitals, 31

Human Rights Council, 72

Hunters Point Shipyard, 74, 75

Hurricane Katrina, 64

Hvistendahl, Mara, 82–86

Hydrogen, 15

I

Ibeanu, Okechukwu, 72

Idaho, 27

Illinois, 8

India, 39, 85

Indian reservations, 20

Indonesia, 9

International Atomic Energy Agency (IAEA), 12, 38, 47

Iodine, 20

Italy, 17

J

James, Revis, 47

Japan
Department of Food Safety Standards, 93

dolphin meat toxicity and, 87–96

Far Sea Fisheries Division of the Resources Management Department, 91–92

Food Safety Division, 92

Hokkaido Health Science University, 91

nuclear waste reprocessing and, 17, 21

Save Japan Dolphins coalition, 91

toxic waste dumping in Philippines, 69–72

Japan External Trade Organization (JETRO), 70

Japan-Philippines Economic Partnership Agreement (JPEPA), 69, 71–72

The Japan Times, 87–88, 91–92

K

Kan Nyu Dai 99 Ban, 93

Katrina (hurricane), 64

Kingery, Ken, 25–29

Kingston Fossil Plant, 79, 81

Knight, Heath, 73–77

Koegler, Sydney, 25

Kondo, Takuya, 93

Kumamoto Medical Science University, 89

L

La Seur, Carrie, 80–81

Landfills, 8

private sector and, 51–63
reprocessing/recycling, 16–18, 21–25, 37, 46, 54
secrecy about, 38
statistics on production of, 53
supercritical fluid technology, 25–28
taxpayer fees for, 57
terrorism and, 11–12, 33, 47
used-fuel management, 55–56, 62–63
See also Low-level nuclear waste; Storage of nuclear waste; Toxic waste; Yucca Mountain
Nuclear Waste Policy Act of 1982, 45–46, 50, 51–53
Nuclear Waste Trust Fund, 46

O

Oak Ridge National Laboratory (ORNL), 83, 86
Obama, Barack, 41, 46, 50, 55
Oil spills, 7, 64
On-site storage of nuclear waste, 32–33
"Open" fuel cycle, 46

P

Perlmutter, David, 91
"Permian Age Rock Salt," 42
PG&E (Pacific Gas and Electric Company), 66, 75
Philippines, 69–72
Philosopher's stone, 14
Pilot whales, 88–89, 93
Plains Justice, 80
Plutonium
    federal dump for, 42

percentage of nuclear waste, 19
radioactivity, 16
reprocessing/recycling, 21, 23–25, 37, 46
Polychlorinated biphenyls (PCBs), 71
Pomerantz, Rachel, 74, 77
Poverty, 72
Pregnant women, 91
Price, Lisa, 49
Princeton University, 23
Private sector management of nuclear waste
    community receptivity issues, 59–60
    current system and, 53–54
    disincentive for waste disposal plans, 51–52
    market-regulated system, 58–59
    nuclear industry reform and, 56–57
    Nuclear Waste Policy Act and, 51–52
    pricing for geologic storage, 57–58
    reprocessing/recycling nuclear waste and, 54–55
    used-fuel management, 55–56, 62–63
    waste disposal fund and, 61–62
    Yucca Mountain management, 60–61
Puig, Max, 90

R

RA 6969 (Toxic Substances and Hazardous and Nuclear Wastes Control Act), 69, 71

DA ODC 2010